Heavenly Portrait:
The Miraculous Image of
Our Lady of Guadalupe

Paul F. Caranci

Visit our website at www.StillwaterPress.com for more information.

First Stillwater River Publications Edition

ISBN-13: 978-1-950339-37-2
ISBN-10: 1-950339-37-8

1 2 3 4 5 6 7 8 9

Written by Paul F. Caranci
Published by Stillwater River Publications, Pawtucket, RI, USA.

Publisher's Cataloging-In-Publication Data
(Prepared by The Donohue Group, Inc.)

Names: Caranci, Paul F., author.
Title: Heavenly portrait : the miraculous image of Our Lady of Guadalupe / Paul
        F. Caranci.
Description: First Stillwater River Publications edition. | Pawtucket, RI, USA :
        Stillwater River Publications, [2019] | Includes bibliographical
        references.
Identifiers: ISBN 9781950339372 | ISBN 1950339378
Subjects: LCSH: Guadalupe, Our Lady of, in art. | Mary, Blessed Virgin, Saint--
        Apparitions and miracles--Mexico. | Conversion--Christianity. |
        Catholic Church--Mexico--History. | Christian art and symbolism--
        Mexico--Modern period, 1500- | Juan Diego, Saint, 1474-1548.
Classification: LCC BT660.G8 C37 2019 N8070 | DDC 232.91/7/097253
704.94855--dc23

Dedication

To Margie,
our children, Heather and Matthew,
and our grandchildren, Matthew, Jr., Jacob, Vincent and Casey.

Acknowledgements

Bringing a book from conception to completion requires the help of many people. I'd like to acknowledge and thank:

Steve and Dawn Porter from Stillwater River Publications for making the process so easy. Sara Benz and the staff at the North Providence Union Free Library who have always been extremely helpful in locating some pretty-hard-to-find reference sources, and accommodating when I needed the material for a bit longer than I initially expected. I appreciate their patience and support. Linda Corsini and Julien Ayotte who help with the tedious task of editing. And, of course, my wife Margie who always provides encouragement, even when she doesn't realize it.

Contents

Preface

Suddenly it was there. The most beautifully detailed self-portrait that Bishop Zumárraga had ever seen. Crafted by the hand of the Mother of God, it was displayed on a cheap cloak worn by a lowly Indian native. A full-color portrait of a pregnant Virgin, so precise in detail that some features wouldn't be detected for five hundred years, and then, only after the discovery of microscopic techniques needed for their revelation.

Like Her Son who, three days following the most tragic day in history some fifteen hundred years earlier, left clear evidence of His resurrection via the impregnation of a photographic negative image on his burial cloth, Mary's semblance is miraculous. So much so that even today, inexplicable detail is being discovered hidden deep within the weave of Juan Diego's tilma which was contrived from the cheapest of cactus fibers.

Unlike the photographic image left by Her Son, however, the portrait of the Blessed Virgin was not intended to capture the most significant moment in history. Rather it was meant to stop injustice and convert a nation of savages who just twenty years earlier had worshiped many bloodthirsty gods at the altar of human sacrifice in rituals so bizarre and heinous that over twenty-thousand people per year, by choice or by force, had their beating hearts ripped from their chests and their bodies dismembered and, in some instances, consumed in cannibalistic frenzy.

And it was, without doubt, the most transformative tool in history, responsible for over eight million conversions in a single decade following the miracle. This miraculous image is also credited with the dedication of a New World to the Catholic faith, a world discovered in 1492 by a young Italian-born sailor by the name of

Christopher Columbus and conquered for Spain by Hernán Cortés in 1521. Spain, the most faithful of Catholic nations at the time, had succeeded in its quest to open the doors of the New World to Catholicism.

Heavenly Portrait: The Miraculous Image of Our Lady of Guadalupe, is the story of God's divine providence, the birth of Catholicism in the Americas, and an image so miraculous that for five hundred years it has withstood destructive natural elements, physical abuse, wars, and intentional attempts at destruction, to remain a sign of the strength and power of God's love for all people and the appointment of His Blessed Mother as protector of all mankind. All that is needed to absorb its power is an open mind and heart.

So, sit back and allow yourself to be transported in time to the new beginnings of a savage nation. Allow your mind to remain open to the endless possibilities and your heart to absorb all the love of the Mother of Life Herself. Enjoy the fascinating story of Our Lady of Guadalupe.

Glossary of Important Names and Places

Alvarez, Eduardo Turati – An ophthalmologist who used the best photographic equipment available, on loan from Kodak, to study the image, concluding that it did not appear to be a painting. Rather, the image had been printed on the tilma.

Aztec Indians – The most dominant natives in central America included some five hundred small states and a population of about five to six million at the height of their power before the Spanish conquest of the 16th century.

Behrens, Helen – A historian who viewed the image without the glass in 1951 and found the colors of the image to be more pronounced when viewed from a distance.

Bernardino, Juan – The Christian name of Juan Diego's uncle whom Diego loved and cared for following the death of his wife. Our Lady appeared to Bernardino on December 12, 1531 and healed him of his affliction. Bernardino died at the age of eighty-six in 1544.

Bonnet-Eymard, Bruno – Examined the eyes at the behest of Dr. Lavoignet. He observed a human bust reflected in both eyes, noting that the image comports to all known optical and ophthalmologic principles.

Bueno, Torroella – An ophthalmologist who reviewed photographs provided by Salines Chávez in 1951 and verified the reflection of the bust of a man with a beard, but in both the left and right eyes of the Virgin. He also noted that the eyes of the Virgin "reacted like the eyes of a live person" when examined.

Cabrera, Miguel – One of Mexico's finest painters. He was one of seven master painters who inspected the tilma in 1751 and determined that the image was a painting, but not one that could have been painted with human hands.

Callahan, Philip Serna – A university professor conducted an infrared analysis of the image in 1979, concluding that there was no trace of paint in the fabric.

Camps Ribera, Francisco – A master painter contracted by Helen Berens in 1954 who was unable to determine the type of paint used in the image. He also noted several heretofore undetected anomalies with the image.

Cataño Wilhelmy, Eduardo – Verified his brother Jesús Cataño Wilhelmy's discovery that the Virgin's face changes colors when viewed at various distances.

Cataño Wilhelmy, Jesús – Photographer who took thirty-four plates of the image with special film that enabled him to distinguish retouched areas from the original image. He also noted that the Virgin's face changes color when viewed at a distance.

Chávez, José Carlos Salinas – Discovered the bust of a man with a beard reflected in the right eye of the Virgin while viewing photographs with a powerful magnifying glass in 1951.

Cuauhlatoa – (Talking Eagle) The given Indian name of Juan Diego used prior to his 1524 baptism into the Christian faith, the time when he officially changed it.

Cuautitlán – The village in which Juan Diego lived with his wife María Lucia.

Codex – Writings of Aztec history considered accurate and reliable by most historians specializing in Aztec history.

Cortés, Hernán – A Spanish conqueror who defeated the Aztec nation for the Spanish Crown. Cortés died on December 2, 1547.

De Bartolache, D. José ph Ignacio – A scholar of medicine and physics who directed two highly accomplished and accredited painters to replicate the image on the tilma in 1787. They were unable to effectively do so.

Diego, Juan – The Indian to whom Our Lady appeared several times over a span of three days in December 1531. Diego died on May 30, 1548.(Cuauhlatoa)

Estremadura – The province in Spain in which the famous Marian Shrine dedicated to Our Lady of Guadalupe is located. In Estremadura, Our Lady of Guadalupe is a statue of the Madonna with Child. The site was a place of worship for Christopher Columbus, Hernán Cortés, Queen Isabel and King Ferdinand of Spain, and Bishop Zumárraga.

Flores, Joaquín – Used high quality photographs in a 1946 study in which he was able to detect staining from embellishments added around the image.

Fuenleal, Sebastián Ramírez de – The bishop of Santo Domingo who was present with Bishop Zumárraga when Juan Diego unfurled his tilma exposing the image of Our Lady.

Gonzales, Alfonso Marcue – Basilica photographer who, in 1929, enlarged photographs taken of the image and discovered a bearded man reflected in the right eye of the Virgin. He also participated in an analysis of the cloth.

Gonzales, Juan – The interpreter for Bishop Zumárraga who was present when Juan Diego exposed the image of the Virgin on his tilma.

Graue, Enrique – A Mexican ophthalmologist who viewed the Virgin's eyes on the image with an endoscope in 1974 and 1975 noting that the image was a supernatural phenomenon.

Gutierrez, Rafael - One of two accomplished and accredited Mexican painters commissioned to replicate the image on the tilma.

Huitzilopochtli – The Aztec god of war, sun, human sacrifice, and the patron of the city of Tenochtitlan.

Ibarra, José de - One of Mexico's finest painters. He was one of seven painters who inspected the tilma in 1751 and determined that the image was a painting., but not one that could have been painted with human hands.

Kuhn, Richard – A biochemist who, in 1936, performed a histological and chemical analysis of the image determining that it contained no synthetic pigments available in 1531.

Kuri, Amado Jorge – A Mexican surgeon studied the image noting that he could detect reflections of people in the Virgin's eyes and that it was like looking into the eyes of a live person.

Lavoignet, Rafael Torija – An ophthalmologist who examined the eyes of the image with an ophthalmoscope that enabled him to see into the fundus of the eye. He observed that the eye was "alive" and nothing like the eyes on paintings by such masters as Raphael, Murillo or Van Dyck.

Llanes, Fernando Ojeda – A Mexican mathematician determined that when the stars and flowers on the mantle were laid across a musical staff, the result was a perfectly harmonious musical melody.

López, Andrés – One of two accomplished and accredited Mexican painters commissioned to replicate the image on the tilma.

María Lucia – The Christian name of the wife of Juan Diego.

Mariscal, Nicolas – Studied the fusion of light and shade on the tilma noting that it had volume as explained by the chiaroscuro effect used by such renowned artists as da Vinci and Caravaggio.

Mesoamerica – The region in the Americas extending from what is now Central Mexico to Belize, Guatemala, El Salvador, Honduras, Nicaragua and northern Costa Rica.

Mestizos - A race of people created by the union (generally by rape) of Mexicans and Aztec Indians.

Mora, Feliciano Cortés Mora – A Basilica abbot who in 1936 commissioned a histological and chemical analysis of the image, determining that it contained no synthetic pigments available in 1531. In 1949 he noted that the cloth was smooth to the touch.

Motolinía, Toribio Fr. – a Franciscan Missionary who was part of the group that baptized as many as six thousand Aztecs in a single day.

Montezuma II, Emperor – (Also known as Moctezuma) was the ninth Tlatoani (ruler) of Tenochtitlan reigning from 1502 to 1520 when he was defeated by Hernán Cortés.

Nahuatl – The native language of the Aztec peoples.

Ochoterena, Isaac – A biologist who with three others analyzed the cloth of the tilma confirming that no sizing was used on the cloth before the image was painted.

Osorio, Manuel - One of Mexico's finest painters. He was one of seven painters who inspected the tilma in 1751 and determined that the image was a painting, but not one that could have been painted with human hands.

Quetzalcoatl – Feathered-Serpent deity of ancient Aztec and Mesoamerican culture.

Ruiz, Patricio Morlete - One of Mexico's finest painters. He was one of seven painters who inspected the tilma in 1751 and determined that the image was a painting, but not one that could have been painted with human hands.

Sánchez, Mario Rojas – A priest who contracted with Dr. Juan Romero Hernán dez Illescas, an astronomer, who examined the alignment of the stars on the tilma and determined that they align with the constellations that appeared in the Mexican sky at exactly the time that Juan Diego unfurled the tilma before Bishop Zumárraga. Even more strange, he noted that it was as if the observer was viewing the stars from above them, not from on earth.

Sánchez, Miguel – Inspected the fabric of the tilma in 1648, discovering that the material was actually two cloaks woven together by a cotton thread.

Taylor, Coley – Discovered a strange and unique phenomenon that causes the image to change in size and color when viewed from different distances.

Tenochtitlan – The capital city of the Aztec nation.

Tepeyac Hill – The site just outside of Mexico City where Our Lady appeared to Juan Diego.

Tilma – The cactus fiber robe worn by Juan Diego upon which the image of Our Lady of Guadalupe appeared on December 12, 1531.

Tlaltelolco – The village in which the Catholic Church attended by Juan Diego and his family was located. It was about fifteen miles from his home in Cuautitlán and about nine miles from Tolpetlac, the village in which Juan Bernardino lived.

Tlaloc – The Aztec god of rain, water, and prosperous earthly fertility.

Tolpetlac – The village in which Juan Bernardino lived.

Tonsmann, José Aste – A Peruvian engineer who observed that the image presents life-like qualities that cannot be reproduced by human hands. Using sophisticated image processing techniques, he also discovered that there were at least four human figures reflected in the eyes of the Virgin.

Tortolero, Manuel Garibi – A researcher who in 1947 examined the photographic plates used by Wilhelmy and concurred with his conclusions that no sizing or preparation of any kind was used on the tilma prior to the image appearing.

Toussaint, Manuel – An art scholar who with three others analyzed the cloth of the tilma to determine its composition.

Vallejo, Francisco Antonio - One of Mexico's finest painters. He was one of seven painters who inspected the tilma in 1751 and determined that the image was a painting, but not one that could have been painted with human hands.

Vega, Luis Lasso de la – Viewed and measured the tilma in 1649.

Velasco, Alfonso Martínez de – Confirmed Jesús Cataño Wilhelmy's discovery that the Virgin's face changes color depending upon the distance from which it is viewed.

Wahlig, Charles – An American doctor, working with his wife Isabelle, who enlarged photographs twenty-five times and noticed two additional human figures reflected in the eyes of the Virgin.

Zumárraga, Don Fray Juan de – A Franciscan Friar who became the Archbishop of Mexico. He established the first printing press in Mexico in 1539. Zumárraga died in 1548.

Introduction

November 14, 1921
Approximately 10:30 in the Morning

As the fortieth President of Mexico from 1924 to 1928, General Plutarco Elías Calles would close and destroy Catholic churches throughout the territory while brutally torturing and killing the parish priests and nuns. One such priest, Father Miguel Pro, displayed the typical courage and faith of all the martyred victims of Elías Calles. Like many, he was led before a firing squad, but prior to collapsing in the hail of bullets, he offered forgiveness with the cry, "Long live Christ the King!"[1]

Plutarco Elias Calles served as the president of Mexico from 1924 to 1928. He was a ruthless, anticleric who burned churches and tortured priests and nuns. On his rise to power, he carried out his intentions in more clandestine ways.

Elías Calles was a devout anti-cleric and a ruthless despot, but on November 14, 1921, his political rise to power with what would become the National Revolutionary Party had only just begun. Until reaching the pinnacle of power in 1924, however, he had no authority to close churches or kill the religious. He was required to settle for more subtle ways to achieve his personal and demented goals.

Minutes before the start of the morning's High Mass, a young man walked slowly, cautiously is perhaps the better word, toward the altar. He labored to carry a large bouquet of flowers as he slowly navigated the center aisle of the Basilica of Our Lady of Guadalupe just outside of Mexico City. He appeared a bit nervous as he approached the altar at the front of the church. Some parishioners recognized him as Luciano Perez Carpio, a factory worker in the city. He was not a regular at daily Mass, and on this day, he was not there to pray, but rather as one in the employ of the private Secretariat of the Presidency.

On November 14, 1921, Luciano Perez Carpio carried a vase of flowers to the altar of the Basilica of Our Lady of Guadalupe. Shortly after his departure, twenty-nine sticks of dynamite hidden in the vase of flowers detonated causing mass destruction. The image of Our Lady, hanging directly above the ground zero, was completely untouched.

At the base of the altar, he genuflected gracefully and looked up at the portrait hanging above him. Then he lowered his vase of flowers to the floor. After a brief moment of silence, he rose and quickly walked away. Minutes later, during the celebration of the High Mass, the bouquet of flowers, so carefully placed in front of the altar, detonated. The explosion was savage, and the terrifying roar could be heard well over a half-mile away. The Basilica's stained glass windows were shattered, as were the windows on other buildings hundreds of yards away from the church. Large vases of flowers around the altar crumbled and the marble steps of the altar, as well as the marble altar rail in front of it, were completely obliterated. In that instant the beautiful sanctuary that lifted the hearts of so many faithful was essentially blown to pieces.

Photo showing the significant damage to The Basilica of Our Lady of Guadalupe shortly after the vase of flowers placed at the altar by Luciano Perez Carpio exploded.

As the dust slowly settled, the stunned parishioners who had assembled to celebrate the Mass checked themselves for injury. Miraculously, no one was seriously hurt. They looked around, taking stock of the damage to their once stunning church. There was so much to take in and their hearts were mellow. Then, as if they all suddenly remembered the treasured painting at the same time, they turned their eyes upward toward the hanging image of Our Lady of Guadalupe. The portrait, which hung just a few feet above the altar, directly above the spot of the planted explosive, was the foundation of the Basilica. The image that had been left on the tilma of a poor Mexican almost four hundred years earlier was a precious relic, the very heart of the Mexican people. It appeared intact, unharmed by the massive detonation that occurred just a few feet below it.

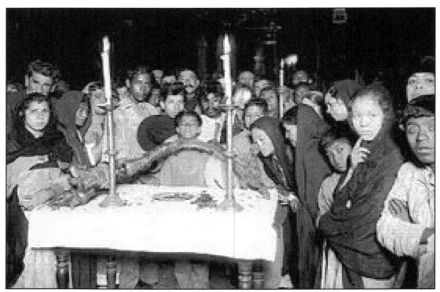

The cast-iron and bronze crucifix that stood on the altar directly under the framed image of Our Lady of Guadalupe. The explosion caused the crucifix to bend at a twenty-degree angle.

The cast-iron and bronze crucifix that stood atop the altar was horribly bent, some 20 degrees backwards toward the tilma as if absorbing the impact from the twenty-nine sticks of dynamite that were hidden in Carpio's vase of flowers, but miraculously, the portrait suffered no visible damage. The thin protective glass of the frame encasing the beautiful image of Our Lady of Guadalupe on the tilma, was not even cracked.

When Our Lady appeared to Juan Diego in 1531, She told the tepid Indian, *"Am I not here, I, who am your Mother? Are you not under My shadow and protection? Are you not in the hollow of My mantle, the crossing of my arms? Am I not the source of all your joy? What more do you need? Let nothing else worry you, disturb you."* On this day, the Virgin Mother once again raised Her compelling arm in testimony to the veracity and power of Her words.

Luciano Perez Carpio entered the Basilica on November 14, 1921 as a fanatical agent of an extreme anti-cleric movement intent on destroying the church and eliminating the sense of hope and joy that it brought to so many. Our Lady, on the other hand, had no intention of allowing that to happen, as "no blast, no temptation, no worry, no evil lurking, is strong enough to harm those in the hollow of Her mantle, in the folding of Her arms."[2] We know this to be true because there is simply no other scientific justification for the prolonged preservation of Her image on the tilma of Saint Juan Diego.

Part I

From Polytheism to Monotheism

Chapter 1
Mesoamerica: A Brief History

The Olmec, an ancient civilization from the tropical low-lands of south-central Mexico, were among the earliest cultures to inhabit the area known as Mesoamerica, the region in the Americas extending from what is now Central Mexico to Belize, Guatemala, El Salvador, Honduras, Nicaragua, and northern Costa Rica. The Olmec reigned from c. 1400 to 400 BCE and were eventually joined or replaced by other groups including the Chiapas, Guatemala, and Oaxaca. Together, these civilizations laid the basis for the Mesoamerican cultural area. In fact, Mesoamerica was in many ways distinguished by an assortment of cultural traits formed and shared by the variety of its indigenous cultures. During this formative period several distinct religions and traditions flourished, as did art and architectural complexes.

The Pre-classic period that followed saw the beginning of Mayan urban polities of a somewhat complex nature. Several political centers sprang up throughout the area. The first Mesoamerican writing systems were developed, peaking with the Mayan hieroglyphics. In only two other regions in the world, Sumer and China, did writing develop so independently, indicating a highly advanced Mayan culture.

A civilization this forward-thinking certainly realized the need for a strong defense against invaders. To that end they developed the city of Teotihuacan, thereby establishing a sort of military and commercial empire that might have been thought invincible.

Nothing lasts forever, though, and in about the year 600 AD, Teotihuacan collapsed, leaving a competition among several rival political centers in central Mexico. It was sometime around the year 1200 that a northern tribe of hunter-gatherers called Aztecs began an emigration from the north, settling in central Mexico. They would come to dominate the political and cultural activities for years to come, even displacing those who spoke the Oto-Manguean languages and instituting their native language of Nahuatl, which would become the dominant language in Mesoamerica by the mid-1350s. By 1325 AD the Aztecs established the basis of their capital city, Tenochtitlan, present day Mexico City, Mexico. The city was unusually large and "boasted a sophisticated and vibrant city centre replete with palaces, elegant residences and imposing temples and pyramids, surrounded by a beautiful lake."[3]

They developed a rather sophisticated agricultural system that included intensive soil cultivation and rudimentary irrigation systems. They also established a powerful military tradition that would enable them to build an empire. They, in fact, were the last great native civilization in pre-Columbian Mesoamerica, "developing an intricate social, political, religious and commercial organization that brought many of the region's city-states under their control by the 15th century."[4]

By the early 16th century, the Aztec empire, either by conquest or trade, included some five hundred small states with a population of five to six million people. The capital city of Tenochtitlan was a bustling center with a population of over one hundred and forty thousand. On a major market day, the city was visited by approximately fifty thousand people. The intense market activity drove the economy of this highly developed social, intellectual and artistic society. The Aztecs also had a strict caste system comprised of nobles at the top and serfs, or indentured servants and slaves, at the bottom.

All the civilizations, from the Olmec to the Aztecs, built pyramids to house their deities and to bury their kings. In many of their great city-states, temple pyramids also fashioned the heart of public life and were the sites of most holy rites including the barbaric ritual of human sacrifice.

The religious rituals of the Aztec civilization included the glorious temples, many palaces, plazas and statues paying tribute to the Aztec gods. Of those, they had many, including the gods of the sun and of war, Huitzilopochtli and Quetzalcoatl, a Toltec god. Additionally, the Aztecs perpetuated, perhaps perfected, the rite of human sacrifice, a practice shared by other religious sects of the time, including the Mayas. The Aztec calendar, which played a significant role in their religious rituals, was based on a solar cycle of 365 days and a ritual cycle that was 105 days less.

While the concept of human sacrifice was not unique to the Aztecs, the distinguishing factor in their performance of the ritual "was the importance with which it was embedded in their everyday life."[5] There are also several distinctive characteristics about the way the Aztecs performed their sacrificial rituals. The Aztec people believed that they owed a blood-debt to the gods and only by satisfying that debt could they hope to avert disaster. Some would cut themselves to offer their blood to the gods. Others would offer animal sacrifices, but when all of this didn't seem to quench the gods' thirst for blood, more was required. Consequently, the Aztec religion was driven by some of the most brutal and merciless forms of human sacrifice known to man. No, human sacrifice was not unique to the Aztec culture, but it seemed to be sharpened by them as they mastered a variety of sacrifices which they used freely throughout the empire.

A depiction of a brutal Aztec human sacrifice during the Festival of Toxcatl, a festival dedicated to the god Tezcatlipoca.

The Aztec sacrifice ritual was very precise and varied slightly depending upon which god was being appeased. Typically, the victim would be painted and taken to the top of the temple or pyramid. Percussion orchestras would lead dancing troops dressed in elaborate costumes performing on carpets of flowers, and with crowds of thousands of commoners and all the elite assembled, four priests would lay the victim on a stone slab called the chacmool. A fifth priest would then use a flint knife to extricate the victim's heart from the chest generally by cutting open the abdomen and then slicing through the diaphragm to access the heart. That same priest would grab the heart, place it in a bowl held by the statue of the honored god. This would be done so quickly that it is said that the victim could sometimes watch the extracted heart beat before succumbing to the trauma. The body would then be cast from the slab and thrown down the steps of the temple or pyramid. Sometimes the body would be fed to zoo animals. Other times the severed head would be placed on display. Frequently, the severed arms and legs would be served at a ceremonial dinner in a cannibalistic ritual.

When the heart wasn't ripped from the chest, victims were sometimes shot with arrows, drowned, burned or otherwise mutilated. At other times victims would be forced to fight to the death, gladiator style. Children were not exempt from the ritual as they were often sacrificed to satisfy the god Tlaloc. Tlaloc was the god responsible for rain, water and prosperous earthly fertility. It was thought that the tears of children were required to mollify this deity.

Though the Aztecs offered their own people in sacrifice, they more often sacrificed their enemies to appease their gods. To ensure an endless stream of people to sacrifice, the Aztecs had special ritual wars called xochiyaoyotl. The object of these wars was not to kill the enemy to gain territory. It was, rather, to capture the enemy as food for the gods. The constant threat of xochiyaoyotl terrified any native not part of the Aztec empire. It is estimated that the number of Aztec sacrifice victims ranged from one thousand to two hundred and twenty thousand per year.

Chapter 2
The Early Explorers
1000 – 1513

Though Christopher Columbus is generally honored as the man who first discovered the "new world," it was Norse explorer Leif Eriksson who may have been the first European "to ever have touched North American soil."[6] Sometime around the year 1000, "Eriksson sailed east to his ancestral homeland of Norway. There, King Olaf I Tryggvason converted him to Christianity and charged him with proselytizing the religion to the pagan settlers of Greenland."[7]

He did indeed convert his mother, who built the first Christian church in Greenland, and others before setting his sights toward exploration.

Sailing in a high-powered Viking wooden ship, the Norseman and his crew of thirty-five Viking sailors departed their native Greenland, ultimately making landfall on the shores of Helluland or

Italian explorer Christopher Columbus, sailing in 1492 under the flag of Spain, discovered the new world. He had a deep devotion to Our Lady even naming his flag ship, Santa Maria, in Her honor.

modern-day Labrador, Canada, before wintering on the northern tip of the island of Newfoundland. There the Vikings discovered a "region abounding with lush meadows, rivers teeming with salmon, and wild grapes so suitable for wine that Eriksson called the region Vinland."[8] Despite North America's more bountiful resources, Eriksson and his men had several adverse and violent encounters with indigenous people there. One such conflict resulted in the death of Eriksson's brother, Thorwald. Consequently, Eriksson and his crew returned to Greenland in the spring and he never left.

Though almost half a millennium had passed since that voyage of Leif Eriksson, accurate recorded history of the Americas and the Caribbean starts with Christopher Columbus. It was his many voyages that "marked the end of thousands of years of isolation between the Western Hemisphere and the rest of the world."[9]

Born in Genoa, Italy in 1451, Columbus was only fourteen when he took his first sea voyage. He studied navigation in Greece and mapmaking in Portugal, but also traveled to Africa, Ireland, England, and Iceland. In 1483 he presented to the kings of Portugal, England, and France his plan to reach the Orient by sailing west across the Atlantic. He had hoped to secure from them the financing he needed to embark on the voyages, but God, it seems, had different plans for the young Christian navigator, as "Catholic Portugal and Spain would serve as the prime instruments used by God in the evangelization of the New World, in particular, South and Central America!"[10]

When the king of Portugal informed Columbus that he would not participate in the proposed voyage, Columbus headed directly for Spain, stopping along the way at the Franciscan monastery of Rabida to pray to his Heavenly Mother for the success of his proposal. By coincidence, or again by divine providence, the Franciscans had a deep interest in navigation and astronomy and were able to offer sound advice to young Columbus prior to his approaching the Queen of Spain. More importantly, "the guardian of the friary had been the Queen's confessor. He provided Columbus with papers introducing him to the Royal Court."[11]

Armed with this new information and door-opening credentials, Columbus made a lasting impression on the Spanish Queen. It is quite providential then that King Ferdinand and Queen Isabella of Spain accepted his offer. Columbus spent the next six years trying to convince them to underwrite the cost of the exploration. Had Spain been torn by the same type of religious dissension that impacted Germany and England at the time of the Protestant revolt, Columbus might have never undertaken his voyages to the New World, but Catholic Spain was to be God's implement in the instruction and conversion of the Americas. Spain had remained deeply religious "while the rest of Europe became more and more secularized in politics, culture and economics. Moreover, the political concept of the Divine Right of Kings was progressively separating Catholic monarchies from the influence of the Church and the Papacy."[12] In addition to "the fact [that] Spain was thoroughly Catholic and thus Marian; the political and economic climate of this country had to be stable and unified [in order to be an effective instrument of God]. All of these improbable conditions existed at the time that Columbus approached the King and Queen of Spain and his "discovery provided the opportunity for the evangelization of millions and the lasting establishment of the Catholic Church in Latin America."[13]

Providence left nothing to chance. When Columbus sought the backing of the King and Queen, Spain had just liberated Granada, freeing the last of the Spanish territory from Moorish domination. There was religious unity in Spain and when "there was a dispute involving accusations of heresy or occult practices, the Inquisition was available to settle it."[14] Queen Isabella shared Columbus's deep devotion and special calling from God to evangelize new worlds in the name of Jesus Christ, and now, she was political free to accommodate his desire. "What Isabella had accomplished in uniting Spain, through just rule, constant vigilance and love of God and her people, made it possible for the Almighty to work out His providential plans for mankind in the discovery of the New World by Christopher Columbus."[15]

Columbus and Queen Isabella were very much alike. "Both were Franciscan tertiaries. Both had a strong devotion to the Blessed Mother. Both were bold leaders who believed strongly in Divine Providence and relied totally on God for the ultimate success of their plans."[16] In fact, while Columbus outfitted his ships and hired his crews, Isabella and Ferdinand "spent two weeks praying at the shrine of Our Lady of Guadalupe in Extremadura, no doubt praying for the success of the bold venture. Columbus also visited the Spanish Guadalupe shrine on a number of occasions. He was an ardent devotee of Our Lady, so much so that he wove her initials into his signature and requested to be buried in her Guadalupe chapel dedicated to the Immaculate Conception."[17] He even named his flagship, *Santa María*, after Her.

Finally, on August 3, 1492, Columbus set sail from Palos, Spain. Each night, as was customary of Catholic mariners, the entire crew gathered to sing *Salve Regina* in honor of the Mother of God. At 2:00 on the morning of October 12, land was sighted. Columbus called the island San Salvador or "Holy Savior." That first voyage also brought Columbus to Haiti and the Dominican Republic, which he called "Hispaniola." There he founded the first European settlement in the Western Hemisphere.

His return journey was not without mishap. Nearing the end of a long, arduous voyage, the tired and worn crew became unnerved when a distinct calmness at sea quelled the sails. The men were near mutiny when Columbus began praying to Mary, Star of the Sea. "A strong wind suddenly blew up, after Columbus had reprimanded the crew for their lack of faith and they prayed to Our Lady. The next day brought additional tension. This time the sea became rough, and strong winds drove the ships on to the great destiny preordained by God. Columbus did not hesitate to write in the ship's log that this 'miracle' was similar to Moses leading the Jews out of captivity. The New World discovery was almost lost on the return journey, when the *Nina* was caught in a most violent storm in the North Atlantic. When the situation worsened and waves were breaking over the frail ship, Columbus called his crew together, vowing a pilgrimage to the Guadalupe shrine in Spain if their lives were spared. He personally fulfilled that vow, barefoot and in sackcloth, after making his report to the Queen.

Before his death at the age of fifty-four on May 20, 1506, Columbus had crossed the Atlantic four times. It wasn't until after the expedition of Vasco Núñez de Balboa in 1513, however, that someone had crossed Central America to reach the Pacific, allowing Europeans to begin to realize the full economic potential of the "New World." Initially, Spain's colonization of this land focused on the islands of the Caribbean. Before long, however, "the lure of wealth spurred Spain's adventures beyond exploration and into a phase of conquest that would lay the foundations of the modern world."[18] The natives of Mesoamerica, however, would not feel the sting of European subjugation until a ruthless vanquisher by the name of Hernán Cortés conquered the Aztec Empire.

Thursday, February 8, 1517 – Saturday, March 3, 1517[19]

The reason for the voyage was somewhat uncertain. Some say it was to capture Indians to be returned to Cuba as slaves. Others insist that the sailors left to discover new lands. Regardless of the motives, about 110 men, including the pilots, boarded three vessels. Two ships of the fleet were warships and the third was a brigantine, a two-masted vessel. Together the restless Spaniards, under the command of Francisco Hernández de Córdoba, left Havana on a quest of discovery and conquest. For twelve days, the three crews followed the coast of Cuba before taking to the open sea on February 20, 1517. Once at sea the crews encountered two continuous days and nights of a furious storm with windswept seas enough to endanger the boats initially while ultimately throwing them off course. Once calm weather was again encountered, the three pilots found themselves driven far from their course.

This was followed by 21 days of calm weather, terminating with the first sighting of land. From their respective ships, according to Bernal Díaz del Castillo, one of the sailors who chronicled the events of the voyage, the crews could see a populated center with many large, solidly built buildings. Having never before seen in Cuba buildings of such stature, the explorers called the land El Gran Cairo. The native Indians referred to it as Catoche.

Chapter 3
The First Europeans Visit Mesoamerica

Sunday, March 4, 1517
Landfall in Catoche

It may not have been their intention to capture the Indians of the Yucatán, but de Córdoba and his men certainly encountered them. No sooner were the ships anchored did inquisitive Indians leave the shore approaching the vessels in pirogues, large canoes powered by both oar and sail. De Córdoba and his men found the Indians to be quite friendly, always smiling and insisting that their foreign visitors join them in their pirogues for the journey back to shore. Once ashore, however, de Córdoba was uneasy at the sight of such a large assembly of natives and began to silently question his safety. The Indians promised to return the next day with even more pirogues to bring the other sailors to shore.

Monday, March 5, 1517

The following day the Indians proved true to their promise and dispatched many pirogues to transfer the remaining sailors from their ships to the shores of Catoche. Intimidated by the large gathering of natives on the shores, the explorers chose to land "en masse using their own launches as a precaution."[20] All seemed to be going well for de Córdoba and his men, but what began as an encounter with seemingly affable natives ended with an ambush perpetrated by the native Chief of El Gran Cairo. As the explorers followed the natives toward the city, the Europeans were attacked by a multitude of Indians, armed with pikes, bucklers, slings, and arrows launched with bows. The stunned Europeans defended themselves using swords, crossbows, and firearms.

Ultimately, the superior weapons used by the Spanish explorers proved too much for the native attackers and the explorers were able to flee, retreat to their ships, and set sail. The battle of Catoche, as the conflict is now known, resulted in the capture of two Indians who would later be baptized into the Roman Catholic faith and serve as interpreters of the Mayan language for the Spanish. It also resulted in the death of two Spaniards.

Tuesday, March 6, 1517 to Tuesday, March 20, 1517
Landfall in Campeche

De Córdoba and his explorers sailed for fifteen days until their drinking water and other supplies had run low, forcing them to make landfall near the Mayan village of Campeche on March 20. There they were greeted by another group of Indians who also appeared to be quite peaceable. With the close call of March 4 still fresh on their minds, however, the Spaniards were understandably suspicious and remained guarded as the men disembarked the ships.

The Indians led their visitors to a solidly built freshwater well, where the travelers were able to fill their casks and jugs to the brim. While in camp, the Spaniards took note of painted figures of serpents on the walls of the well-constructed shelters and were also introduced to their first Mayan priests. The priests donned white tunics and stood by a newly lit fire. It was readily apparent to the incredulous visitors that the priests' long dark hair had been impregnated with human blood, something they suspected to be a ritualistic omen.

It was then that the Indians' attitudes seemed to change, and they informed the Spanish interlopers that if they did not depart by the time the fire went out, they would be beaten. Having already experienced the ferocity of one attack, the explorers wasted no time in their departure from Campeche.

Wednesday, March 21, 1517 to Friday, March 30, 1517

Safely aboard their ships, the Spaniards set sail once again. This time, however, the weather was as uncertain as the mood of the Indians. Following six days of smooth sailing, the sailors found themselves in the throes of a four-day-long tempest that almost caused their ships to sink. Though they survived the storm, the delay created yet another drain on their supplies, requiring them to stop once again to fill their drinking casks and jugs.

Saturday, March 31, 1517
Landfall at Champotón

Their arrival was uninterrupted by Indians and they disembarked freely, searching for, and quickly finding, a source of potable fresh water. After filling their jugs, however, they noticed that they were surrounded by "great assemblies of Indians,"[21] and immediately realized the peril. This time, though, the prospect of flight seemed more dangerous than that of attack, so they decided to maintain their position and fight. The night was a sleepless one as they anticipated an attack under the cover of darkness. It never came.

Sunday, April 1, 1517
The "Evil Battle" of Champotón

The peace that characterized the night was broken at morning's first light, signaling the start of a brutal engagement. Daylight also revealed the stark reality that the Spaniards were massively outnumbered, possibly as much as two hundred to one. Within minutes, eighty Spaniards fell wounded, leaving only twenty or so men still able to fight. To make the situation even more perilous, not all the able-bodied men were trained in the art of fighting. The Indians, meanwhile, had a constant flow of fresh reinforcements and all of them seemed to be targeting the Spanish leader. Hernández de Córdoba was hit by ten arrows and two of the survivors were captured to be offered as a sacrifice to the gods.

The men, only one of whom was unhurt at this point, made a wise decision to retreat, withdrawing on short order to the ships which they were surprised to find still intact. The Indians followed them to the shore, from which point they attacked the retreating ships with arrows, stones, and pikes. Some of the survivors were forced to abandon the ships, either swimming or hanging on to the edges of the launches.

In all, about fifty men were lost in the battle including the two that were taken captive as intended sacrifices to the gods. Of the survivors who escaped to safety, many of whom were badly injured, five died and were buried at sea in the days following the escape. There were not even enough healthy men left to pilot and staff three ships, forcing them to first salvage any usable material from one of the ships and then set it afire on the high sea.

Some of the explorers managed to escape the horrors of Champotón, though for years the Spanish would refer to the area as the "Coast of the Evil Battle." This name even appeared on Spanish maps of the time.

During the voyage, according to del Castillo, their "thirst became intolerable...and their mouths and tongues were cracked." A decision was made to navigate to Florida to obtain some much-needed water before completing their journey to Cuba. The two ships anchored off San Carlos Bay and the men rowed ashore where they were once again attacked by Indians, this time the Calusa tribe. The engagement resulted in the disappearance of one man and the wounding of six others. Thirty-five Indians were killed before the Spaniards were able to fill their casks with water sufficient to complete the journey. The explorers collected their wounded and the water jugs and boarded their ship for the final time before reaching their destination.

Despite the fresh water supply, one more man expired along the way and de Córdoba himself along with three other men, succumbed to mortal wounds received during the battle of Champotón, just days after disembarking in San Cristóbal, Cuba. Though de Córdoba's life was ended, his experiences with the Indians of Mesoamerica lived on in stories told and retold by the survivors and in diaries that were kept by some of the sailors. These stories certainly colored the minds of future explorers who were much more guarded in their endeavors and certainly better prepared to undertake military-type entanglements with the natives they encountered.

The Yucatán Conquistador

Hernán Cortés was highly intelligent and greatly inspired by the recent voyages of Columbus, and his impression of the native population of Mesoamerica was tainted by stories he heard about the earlier voyages of de Córdoba. Satisfying his desire for the adventurous life of a conquistador, Cortés left Spain in 1504 to travel to Hispaniola, where he became an influential figure in the newly formed colonial government. In 1511 he joined an expedition to conquer Cuba and developed skills that would serve him well in his career. It was in 1518, however, that Cortés was appointed to lead an exploratory expedition to Mexico, one that he, in violation of his orders, would turn into a historic military conquest.

The ruthless conquistador, Hernán Cortéz, overcame the Aztec strength defeating Moctezuma II in a relatively short period of time, but his conversion efforts were equally brutal and not nearly as successful.

Arrival in Mesoamerica
February 1519

With a fleet of eleven ships that carried one hundred sailors, five hundred soldiers, and sixteen horses, Cortés made landfall in Mesoamerica in February 1519 and began a mission that resulted in the "swift and spectacular decline"[22] of the Aztec Empire and the end of the reign of Emperor Moctezuma II, also known as Montezuma.

Moctezuma II was a ruthless leader. During his reign of power, which lasted from about 1502 to 1520, he initiated bloody conquests of many of the surrounding territories, greatly expanded the size of the temple and exponentially increased the number of ritualistic human sacrifices.

Upon his arrival, Cortés quickly imposed control over the indigenous population along the coast, resulting in the acquisition of twenty slaves gifted him by the local chieftain. One among the slaves became vital to Cortés, serving as both his interpreter and mistress.

Before long, the news of the arrival of Cortés began to spread quickly, reaching the ears of Emperor Moctezuma in Tenochtitlan. Perhaps as a means of "taming the beast," the Emperor sent gifts of gold to the interloper, but rather than appeasing Cortés, the gifts inflamed his cravings for more Aztec riches. Cortés knew he would remain and conquer the land, but in case his troops had other thoughts, he "ordered the total destruction of the fleet he had sailed with from Cuba. There was now no turning back."[23]

Cortés and his men marched toward Tenochtitlan, observing and manipulating local political rivals along the way. He won a military victory over a group of natives called the Tlaxcaltec and gained the support of the Totonac peoples from the city of Cempoala, who hoped to be freed from the Aztec yoke. With each victory Cortés increased the size of his army. "Knowledge of the divisions among different native peoples, and an unerring ability to exploit them, was central to Cortés's strategy."[24]

The Spanish leader also had little tolerance for dissenters, which he defined as anyone loyal to Moctezuma. Upon learning that the holy city of Cholula joined with the Emperor in an attempt to slow the advance of the invaders, Cortés ordered his men to unleash a punishing attack on the city that lasted two days.

"To Cortés and the men who fought with him, religion was as much a part of the practical side of living as breathing."[25] It was a display of his faith that prompted him to bring on the voyage, "several small wooden statues of the Virgin which could rightly be called the 'Madonnas of Cortés.'"[26] It is not surprising, therefore, that one of the Aztec practices that most disturbed Cortés was the concept of human sacrifice. It was the source of much of his concern regarding the indigenous people of Mesoamerica and a topic that he addressed frequently in his letters. In one such letter he wrote:

> "They have a most horrid and abominable custom which truly ought to be punished and which until now we have seen in no other part, and that is that, whenever they wish to ask something of the idols, in order that their pleas may find more acceptance, they take many girls and boys and even adults, and in the presence of these idols they open their chests while they are still alive and take out their hearts and entrails and burn them before the idols, offering the smoke as sacrifice. Some of us have seen this, and they say it is the most terrible and frightful thing they have ever witnessed."[27]

Conquest of Tenochtitlan
November 1519

Cortés seemed unstoppable and Moctezuma didn't know how to respond. With Tenochtitlan's 250,000 inhabitants, Cortés was outnumbered two hundred and fifty to one. Regardless, the King essentially allowed "the Spaniards and their allies to enter Tenochtitlan unopposed in November 1519," rousing fear in the hearts of all those living in the Aztec capital. Cortés thought himself invincible now and quickly captured Moctezuma. He took control of the palace, reducing Moctezuma to puppet-king status.

8Aztec King Moctezuma II was captured by Cortez, who took control of the Aztec palace, reducing the shamed leader to puppet-king status.

With the conquest behind him, and riches beyond his imagining in hand, Cortés hoped for a peaceful transition of power with the Aztec people, but peace was not a commodity within his grasp.

Diego Velázquez, the Cuban governor who had appointed Cortés to lead a peaceful expedition to Mexico, was enraged by Cortés's reckless insubordination and ordered a punitive expedition to Mesoamerica to deal with the situation. Consequently, in early 1520, Cortés was forced to depart the city to battle with his own people. Taking the majority of his army, Cortés "left Tenochtitlan under the command of Pedro de Alvarado and a garrison of eighty Spaniards."[28]

This, as it turned out, was a mistake. Alvarado lacked leadership skills and was easily angered. When Cortés returned to Tenochtitlan on June 24, following the defeat of the Velázquez expedition forces, he found the city in rebellion. Alvarado had executed so many Aztec chiefs that the people rose up in revolt. The Spaniards tried to use Moctezuma to calm the people, but they stoned their former king, delivering injuries from which he died a few days later. The revolt escalated and "on June 30, 1520, the Spanish fled the city under fire, suffering hundreds of casualties. Some Spaniards died by drowning in the surrounding marshes, weighed down by the vast amounts of treasure they were trying to carry off. The event would come to be known as the Night of Sorrow."[29]

The Spaniards did return to the city however, and ultimately, a smallpox epidemic among the Aztec people and the advanced Spanish weaponry proved to be too much for the Aztecs to overcome, despite their superior numbers. "'On a sudden, they speared and thrust people into shreds,' wrote one indigenous chronicler, having witnessed the terrifying impact of European arms. 'Others were beheaded in one swipe...Others tried to run in vain from the butchery, their innards falling from them and entangling their very feet.'"[30]

The war lasted some fourteen months, with ultimate conquest declared on August 13, 1521. Victory was total and brutal, leaving the Aztecs crushed. The Spaniards captured a great many enemy combatants to be used as slaves. So many were captured, in fact, that the newly indentured, some of whom were branded following their seizure, now outnumbered the fighting Spaniards. One witness wrote, "Not a single stone remained left to burn and destroy."[31]

Both in total figures and in its disproportionality, the loss of life was astounding. During the fourteen months of the siege of Tenochtitlan, the Aztecs lost as many as one hundred thousand people compared to the loss of only one hundred Spaniards. In the end, Cortés proved both ruthless and cunning, but his efforts had certainly transformed Mesoamerica. The conquest of Mesoamerica was a critical stage in the Spanish colonization of the Americas.

Any conquest will produce unintended consequences. One such outcome in the conquest of the Aztecs was the introduction of a mixed race of people known as the Mestizos. In the conquest of Mesoamerica by the Spanish, Spaniard men impregnated, generally by rape, Indian women. The Spanish saw the resulting children as the fruits of war and debauchery. The Aztecs saw them as the consequences of rape. Accordingly, the Mestizos were held with the greatest contempt by both peoples. They were unwanted and abandoned in large numbers. Even the local bishop "noted that orphans, the children of Spaniards and Indian women, wandered around homeless, eating whatever they could find, even raw meat."[32]

Chapter 4
The Era of Conversion
1521 to 1539

Virtually from the moment of Cortés's arrival in Mesoamerica in February of 1519 through the fall of Tenochtitlan on August 13, 1521, the Spaniards and the Aztecs were at war. "The Aztecs fought to preserve their traditions and their way of life while the Spanish waged a spiritual crusade, hoping to win souls to the faith, land for the Spanish crown, and large amounts of gold,"[33] and to that end, shortly after the fall of Tenochtitlan, the "Spanish conquerors began the gradual process of converting the Aztecs to Christianity."[34]

Within a relatively short time, tens of thousands of Aztecs were converted to Catholicism. It is widely thought that a combination of three distinct scenarios brought about the conversions. First, the Aztecs, a culture steeped in superstition, suspected that the conquistadors were gods returning to claim their land. Second, there was a degree of intimidation used in preaching Catholicism to the Aztecs. Finally, the Spanish missionaries may have blended the Aztec and Christian religions to ease the conversion of the Aztec people.

Indeed, these theories have their basis in fact. Bernal Díaz de Castillo, one of the Spanish soldiers "under the command of Cortés, wrote that Moctezuma spoke to him and to the other Spaniards saying, 'his ancestors in years long past had spoken, saying that men would come from where the sun rose to rule over these lands, and that we must be those men...' In other words, this was a confirmation that Moctezuma believed Cortés and his men to be deities."[35] Other writings found in the Forentine Codex, a compilation of Aztec history as told by the natives, also verifies through various other sources that "the appearance of Cortés resembled the description of [the god] Quetzalcoatl."[36] Alexia Dovas wrote in the Lambda Alpha Journal at Wichita State University, "...because some of the Aztecs believed Cortés was truly a god they obeyed and converted to Catholicism as Cortés instructed them to do so. This was known as 'the year when the faith came.'"[37]

Despite the evidence for mistaken identity, Cortés still needed to exert a great deal of force in his attempts to convert the Aztec people. He and most Spaniards believed that it was their duty as servants of God and to the King and Queen of Spain to convert Aztecs to Catholicism. This was evident in the earliest conversations between Cortés and the Emperor. "After Cortés became aware that Moctezuma thought he was Quetzalcoatl, Cortés asked about converting Moctezuma. Because the Emperor did not reply and since there was resistance by the Aztecs to convert, Cortés began to take power in his own hands. This resulted in the destruction of the Aztec idols and temples. In Cortés' Second Letter to the Spanish King, Cortés wrote, 'The most important of these idols, and the ones in whom they have most faith, I had taken from their places and thrown down the steps...' Later in the same letter, Cortés wrote that 'the idols were taken away and the altars were cleared of the blood.' The idols were replaced with images of the Virgin Mary."[38]

The destruction of Aztec temples and their many icons to false gods led to some initial resistance. The Aztec people wept at the sight of their idols being destroyed and when attempting to resist this destruction through rebellion, the rebels were killed by Spanish conquerors as were many of the kings and princes of neighboring cities. "As one native wrote to the king of Spain, '[the people of] many towns were forced and tortured, were hanged or burned, because they did not want to leave idolatry, and unwillingly they received the gospel and faith.' Out of fear, the Aztecs reluctantly saw no other way but to convert."[39]

The final and most recent theory describes a voluntary conversion of the indigenous people resulting from the similarities between Catholicism and the Aztec religion. Despite the many and obvious distinctions between the two religions, the similarities were several.

For example, both religions shared the cross as a symbol. To the Catholics, the cross is a symbol of redemption while the Aztecs used it as a symbol for the god of rain. Additionally, each religion venerated a female figure. In Catholicism that woman is obviously the Virgin Mary. For the Aztecs, it was Tonantzin "our mother" who "was revered as the goddess of fertility of life (human and agriculture). Other shared common religious practices were baptisms, confessions, communions, feast days, and fasting."[40]

The Aztecs regarded baptism as a way to purify one's soul. Consequently, many were anxious to convert to Catholicism and undergo this sacrament. Writing for the Franciscan missionaries, Fr. Gante [Fray Pedro de Gante] noted that the missionaries baptized "eight thousand, sometimes ten thousand, and even fourteen thousand persons in one day."[41]

It is also probable that the Aztecs found the Catholic sacrament of confession more appealing to their own. The Aztec religion enabled sinners to confess a particular sin only one time with the possibility of godly forgiveness. Each successive offense of the same type could not be forgiven. The Catholic practice of forgiving the same sin multiple times was one the Aztec people found alluring.

The missionaries sensed that the key to the successful conversion of the native population was contained within the exploitation of familiar practices. "The friars believed that if the Aztec traditions, that were similar to the Christian traditions, were combined, it would seem more appealing for the Aztecs to convert."[42] For that reason, the missionaries learned the native language of Nahuatl and the intricacies of their religion. They found a way to join the common elements of the two religions, the product of which became known as "Nahua Christianity."[43] In that way, the Aztecs "took what they considered fundamental Christian rites and still maintained the basic Nahua traditions."[44]

The Franciscan Friars even built their churches where the Aztec temples once stood, enabling the indigenous peoples to continue to worship in the same location. The amalgamation of the two different religions, cultures, and schools of thought resulted in the conversion of tens of thousands of Aztecs into the Catholic faith.

Cortés, however, could not have converted the Aztecs alone, even employing the tactic of conversion by destruction, and relied heavily on the missionaries to take up the mantle of that charge. Since 1523, Franciscan Fray Pedro de Gante[45] had been evangelizing in the region as part of Cortés's entourage. Cortés preferred missionaries of the Mendicant tradition since they shared a strong commitment to poverty. They essentially "had in principle renounced all worldly goods and were less likely to compete with Spanish conquerors for land and resources,"[46] since their only goal was the salvation of souls through evangelization and conversion.

The missionaries faithful to the Mendicant tradition included the Franciscan, Dominican, and Augustinian orders. These missionaries shared a strong commitment to the poor as they themselves were called to a life of poverty. Resultingly, the Order's founding principles state, "...the brothers shall appropriate nothing to themselves, neither a place nor anything; but as pilgrims and strangers in the world, serving God in poverty and humility, they shall with confidence go seeking alms. Nor need they be ashamed, for the Lord made himself poor for us in this world. This is that summit of most lofty poverty which made you, my most beloved brothers, heirs and kings of the kingdom of heaven."[47] The Mendicant orders were established in the 13th century "by men who rejected the opulent and decadent lifestyles of Catholic churchmen and their lack of education."[48] They believed that "wealth inevitably corrupts Christians and leads them away from a lifestyle pleasing to God."[49] They preached that a good Christian is one that imitates the "life of the disciples of Jesus as revealed in the Gospels: a life of poverty devoted to evangelizing the unconverted in which the missionaries were supported by alms."[50]

This emphasis on poverty led the orders to appreciate the simple living conditions of the Aztec people and even considered the native way of life superior to the "Spanish culture because it seemed to be uncorrupted by money and greed, in perfect harmony with their own ideal of poverty."[51] The early missionaries, in fact, had grand visions of building an Indian church in Mesoamerica that "would not be contaminated with the perverted church of Europe."[52]

The first group of Mendicant missionaries, the Franciscans, arrived in Mesoamerica on either June 17 or 18 in 1524. Joining Fray Pedro de Gante were a group of twelve missionaries, led by Fray Martín de Valencia, that would become known as the "Twelve Apostles of Mexico."[53] Although led by de Valencia, the most famous of the twelve was Fray Toribio de Benavente Motolinía, who wrote extensively on the customs of the Nahuas and the challenges of Christian evangelization. His writings have become an essential historical resource for this period in Mexican history.

Oddly, it was the Spanish Crown and not the Catholic Church that funded the missionary activities in Mesoamerica. "Spain paid for the journey of missionaries to America, for missionary expeditions within America and a yearly stipend for the maintenance of mission stations. The financial and administrative dependence of the Catholic Church in colonial Mexico on the Spanish Crown made the church an arm of the colonial state."[54]

This arrangement was not without benefit to Spain, nor was it unbeneficial to the church. For the Spanish Crown, evangelization legitimized its conquest of new lands and the subjugation of the people of those lands. "In exchange for Spain's pledge to convert the American peoples to Catholicism, Pope Alexander VI officially approved of the conquest of America by the Spanish....Spain's undertaking was declared to be legitimate by what was then Europe's highest moral authority and the Roman Catholic Church gained an unimagined number of new adherents at a time when the Reformation dramatically challenged its influence in Europe."[55]

Among the first in the region to be baptized into the Catholic faith by the Twelve Apostles of Mexico was a fifty-year-old native of Cuautitlán by the name of Juan Diego Cuauhlatohuac.[56] Diego was born in Mexico in 1474 and was raised in accordance with the Aztec pagan religion by his uncle, Juan Bernardino, following the early death of Juan Diego's father. In 1524 Diego and his wife María Lucia, the names taken upon their baptism, converted to Catholicism and after their baptism became very committed to their new lives. They would often walk long distances for the opportunity to learn about the faith at the Franciscan mission station at Tlatelolco.

The Franciscan missionaries were not alone in Mesoamerica for too long a time. The Dominican Friars joined them two years later in 1526 and the Augustinian missionaries several years after that in 1533. Together they established a glut of missions throughout the region totaling 942. The Franciscans led the way with 610 missions. The Dominicans established 192 and the Augustinians 140.

The Franciscan Friars were the first missionaries to reach Mexico following the fall of Moctezuma. Though they were followed by the Dominican and Augustinian missionaries, the number of conversions still fell below one million after a ten-year effort.

The mission stations did not have a singular purpose. In addition to serving as the heart of religious conversion, they "also contributed to the economic and cultural conquest of the native population."[57] Within just a few years, some seventy Franciscan houses were established in Mexico and they became a vital instrument in the religious education of the new Catholic converts.

Following the approval of King Charles V of Spain, Tenochtitlan's Archbishop Juan Zumárraga established the first printing press in Mexico City in 1539. Under the direction of Italian printer Juan Pablos, religious publications were printed in twelve languages and distributed throughout the region, greatly assisting in the conversion of tens of thousands of Aztecs natives. Despite the successes of the Mendicant missionaries, "conversion of the natives remained a slow and uphill process. Then something quite extraordinary happened which irreversibly changed the course of Mexican history and civilization."[58]

Part II

Juan Diego

Chapter 5
A Study in Humility

Cuauhtlatoa (Talking Eagle), from the Chichimeca tribe, was born in 1474 in Cuautitlán, a village about fifteen miles northeast of Tenochtitlan. Fifty-seven years later, however, his homeland was hardly recognizable. Over the course of his life his native Mexico had been transformed, as was Cuauhtlatoa himself. Neither he nor his Aztec nation were the same. Many gods had been reduced to the one true God. Human sacrifices were a thing of the past, and Jesus Christ had replaced Huitzilopochtli, Quetzalcoatl, and other gods as the center of his family's faith. Since his conversion and baptism into the Catholic Church by the Franciscan missionaries in 1524, Cuauhtlatoa assumed his Christian name, Juan Diego. He had become a very religious man with a deep devotion to the Virgin Mary, the Mother of Jesus.

Juan Diego, a humble Indian Catholic convert was walking to Mass in celebration of the Feast of the Immaculate Conception when the melodic sound of music drew him up Tepeyac Hill. There he had the first of four encounters with the Blessed Virgin who sent him to the bishop with a special message.

Ten years had passed since the conquest of the capital city of Tenochtitlan. The "arrows and shields were put down; everywhere the inhabitants of the lake and the mountain had surrendered. Thus, faith started; it gave its first buds; and it flowered in the knowledge of the One through Whom We Live, the true God, Téotl."*

Change is not always good, and it is seldom accepted without resistance. But for Juan Diego, his wife María Lucia, and his uncle Juan Bernardino who was also baptized into the faith, life seemed better since the Spanish conquered and converted the territory. Unlike most Aztec Indians who were polytheistic, Juan Diego was from a region that was under the influence of the kingdom of Texcoco, part of a triple alliance with Tlacopan and Tenochtitlan. Nezahualcoyotl, the king of Texcoco from 1402 to 1472, rejected the polytheism of his contemporaries and was of the belief that there was only one, albeit unknown, God. The king also rejected human sacrifice, but to appease his subjects, he allowed the practice using only prisoners of war in the barbaric rituals. It is most probable, therefore, that Juan Diego was already familiar with the concept of monotheism and therefore more acceptant of Christianity.

For Diego life had not been easy. After losing his parents while still a young child, Juan was raised by his uncle with whom he lived until his marriage to María Lucia. The couple moved to Cuautitlán where they lived in a small, one-room mud house, the roof of which was thatched with corn stalks.

Diego had no real profession. He was, rather, a jack-of-all-trades whose farming, furniture-making, and weaving skills did not amount to a good living. Consequently, he hired himself out to anyone in the area looking for a helping hand.

In addition to his home in Cuautitlán, Juan Diego also owned a house and some land in Tolpetlac, the village of his uncle Juan Bernardino, which is about six miles south of Cuautitlán. Because

---

* *Note: According to* https://findwords.info/term/teotl, **Téotl** *is a central idea of Aztec religion. The Nahuatl* **term** *is often translated as "god," but it may have held more abstract aspects of the numinous or divine, akin to the Polynesian concept of Mana. In Pipil mythology Teut (Nawat cognate of **Téotl**) is known merely as the creator and the father of life.*

he owned two homes and some land and had a rudimentary education, Juan was considered middle class by most who knew him, though in reality he was generally poor his entire life.

Physically, Juan Diego was rather small, and though friendly, remained very reserved. He was also humble and even walked with a stoop as if not worthy. He could frequently be seen with his wife shuffling the fifteen-mile, one-way trip to Tlaltelolco, "to attend Mass and receive the Sacraments and further instruction in the Faith. They would rise long before dawn to begin the long journey on foot over the hills, for the missionaries had stressed the importance of arriving early for Mass."[59] The distance of the walk was not unusual for Juan and his wife. They had taken hundreds, if not thousands, of journeys of similar distance since childhood. Now, however, with his advancing age and the undulant nature of the terrain, that distance was taking its toll. Regardless, Juan didn't mind the painful trek to the Franciscan convent because he greatly enjoyed the religious education and stories that the Friars would impart, and he took comfort in the "contrast between the horrors of paganism and the love, joy, and vibrant hope of Christianity [which] could not have been more absolute."[60] Upon arrival he and María Lucia lowered themselves onto the hard ground just as did hundreds of other Mexicans there for the same purpose.

1529

This was the new life of Juan Diego. Simple and poor, but happy with the loving companionship of María Lucia in the comforting presence of a forgiving God. That is until the tragic day on which his precious María Lucia suddenly died. Juan was understandably devastated. Without a child of his own, he now found himself grieving in an empty house. No one sitting beside him at the dinner table or spinning the loom. He found the evenings particularly intolerable as each minute of solitude and soulful reminiscence must have seemed like hours.

Unwilling to tolerate the desolation any longer, Juan packed his things and moved to Tolpetlac to be near his aging uncle. The new location had the added advantage of being only nine miles from the church in Tlaltelolco, saving significant time and adding to his daily productivity.

At the new house, Juan passed the time cultivating his gardens of corn and beans. He would occasionally hunt for venison and was able to spend a great deal of time with the uncle he so loved. Diego had a very special bond with his uncle and now had the time to care for him as he wanted. Of course, he continued to attend Mass, traversing the miles of hilly terrain just as before, only now, he did so alone in the pre-dawn darkness. Juan Bernardino's advanced age prevented him from accompanying his nephew to Mass, and the loneliness of the long walk was surely not easy for the man who had so many fond memories of his walks and discussions with María Lucia.

The Feast of the Immaculate Conception
Saturday, December 9, 1531*

Juan rose earlier than most days to ensure his arrival at Mass. There was an undeniable chill in the air as the nine-mile journey commenced under the cover of starlit skies. It was the Feast of the Immaculate Conception[61] and Juan was to assist in the celebration of "Mass in honor of his Mother and his Queen."[62]

Although we now use the Gregorian calendar, the Julian calendar was used in 1531, the days of the week noted in describing the events as they happened to Juan Diego are those of the Julian calendar. The dates are the same, but the discrepancies in the days of the week are many. For example, the Julian calendar lists December 9, 1531 as a Saturday, though December 9 falls on a Wednesday on the Gregorian calendar. For the sake of consistency, the events in the life of Juan Diego are noted using the days of the Julian calendar.

For Juan, this feast had a special significance ever since he first learned about Mary's role in the faith. On this day, however, with the melancholy feeling of loss and desolation, it took on an even greater significance, because "the all-pure and shining one, celestial Queen of Heaven, was his own personal Mother." A mother who could comfort him like no one else on earth could. As he thought about Her, his pace quickened. The miles of rolling hills and rocky trails seemed less burdensome now, as did the cold wind that snapped across his cheeks.

The Virgin Mary Appears to Juan Diego

As he approached the base of Tepeyac hill to his east, the site of the former pagan temple of Tonantzin, he heard the faint sounds of music. He stopped to listen more closely, but, deducing that it was just his imagination, he continued. With each additional step, however, the music, the most beautiful melodic sound he had ever heard, became more pronounced. As Juan stared at the hill of Tepeyac he noticed a "glowing white cloud, emblazoned by a brilliant rainbow formed by rays of dazzling light streaming from the cloud."

The music stopped but the momentary silence was broken by the sound of someone calling out to him. The soft, soothing voice of a woman came from the summit of the hill. *"Juanito...Juan Dieguito,"* she called using the diminutive of his name in the most courteous and reverent of ways.

Juan looked to the top of the incline but saw nothing. Unafraid, he climbed the rocky hill one hundred and thirty feet to the summit where he came "face to face with a Lady of overpowering brilliance and beauty. Her garments shone like the sun and the radiance of her person snuffed the surrounding rocks, mesquite bushes, prickly pears, and other scrubby plants growing nearby, spangling them with a riot of color, as if they were being viewed through the stained-glass windows of some magnificent cathedral."[63]

The Lady, a girl really of about fourteen, beckoned Juan to come closer. He advanced several paces and then fell to his knees in veneration. *"Juanito, my son, where are you going?"* she asked in the most gracious of tones. "Noble Lady," Juan replied, "I am on my way to church in Tlaltelolco to hear Mass." The Lady smiled approvingly and said,

> *"Know for certain in your heart, my most abandoned son, that I am the Ever-Virgin Holy Mary, Mother of the God of Great Truth, Téotl, of the One through whom We live, the Creator of Persons, the Owner of what is near and together, of the Lord of Heaven and Earth. I very much want and ardently desire that my hermitage be erected in this place. In it I will show and give to all people all my love, my compassion, my help and my protection, because I am your merciful mother and the mother of all the nations that live on this earth who would love me, who would speak with me, who would search for me, and who would place their confidence in me. There I will hear their laments and remedy and cure all their miseries, misfortunes, and sorrows. And for this merciful wish of mine to be realized, go there to the palace of the bishop of Mexico, and you will tell him in what way I have sent you as messenger, so that you may make known to him how I very much desire that he build me a home right here, that he may erect my temple on the plain.*
> *You will tell him carefully everything you have seen and admired and heard. Be absolutely certain that I will be grateful and will repay you; and because of this I will make you joyful; I will give you happiness; and you will earn much that will repay you for your*

trouble and your work in carrying out what I have entrusted to you. Look, my son, the most abandoned one, you have heard my statement and my word; now do everything that relates to you."[64]

The Virgin Mary, appearing to Diego as a pregnant fourteen-year-old girl, told Juan to pick the flowers growing on this December day and bring them to the bishop as the sign he had requested.

Juan bowed his head and lowered his body to the ground and answered, "My Owner and my Queen, I am already on the way to make your statement and your word a reality. And now I depart from you, I your poor servant."[65] Then he turned and descended the hill in the direction of the road that led to Mexico City.

Surrounding and weaving through the city were five inter-connected lakes. Though Lakes Zumpango, Xaltocan, Texcoco, Xochimilco, and Chalco covered some 2,000 square miles of land, the Aztecs had managed to build around them a remarkable arrangement of dams and causeways. This ingenious people also fashioned an archipelago of floating islands, called chinampas (floating gardens) on which indigenous fruits and vegetables were planted and nurtured, supplementing the dietary needs of the city's inhabitants.

Juan made his way toward the city. He was certain of what he saw and certainly understood his Lady's request, but he was confused by the whole encounter. As the sun began its natural ascent, replacing the blackness of night with the deep shades of blue that now illuminated the sky, many questions swirled in Juan's head. Why would the Mother of God appear to him? He wasn't important. How could he possibly convince the bishop to build a church? Would he even be allowed to meet with the bishop at this hour or any hour? He also relived the words of his Queen and Mother, repeating them to himself many times. She had chosen Her words carefully and spoke directly to him. She used a litany of names by which She identified Herself. This was a most important revelation because they are the same names noted by "Nahuatl theologians in their dialogues with the Spanish theologians and that were discredited by the Spanish evangelizers. They appeared in the purest preconquest theology of the Nahuatls."[66] In using these words, Mary reestablishes the authenticity and truth of these holy names, indicating that these "names refer to neither demons nor false idols; they are venerable names of God."[67] She also employed use of the word "hermitage," which could refer to an orphanage, a place for the homeless, and a hospice, all places for a "people who had been totally displaced and left homeless by conquest."[68] The Lady, in fact, used a progression of words to describe what she wanted to have built to her honor starting with "hermitage," a place of affectionate relationships for the homeless, and progressing to "temple," a manifestation of the sacred. These words and phrases were carefully chosen to make Juan feel comfortable. All along the route to Mexico City and even upon entering the city, Juan's head was abounding with uncertainties and admiration.

Juan Diego Meets with the Bishop

Approaching the bishop's residence, Juan knocked on the door. It opened slowly until Diego was looking at a bewildered servant carefully studying the unkempt appearance of the stranger standing on the stoop outside. Juan asked, in his typically humble way, to see the bishop. The servant was suspicious and just stared at Juan as he repeated his request. Oddly, the servant stepped aside and told the visitor to take a seat on the patio while he beckoned the bishop.

Time passed, at least an hour, though it seemed to Juan to be much longer. He was cold and uncomfortable, but he had been assigned a task by the Mother of God and would not evade his responsibility. Wrapping his tilma around his body even tighter, he lowered his head to avoid the wind snapping at the exposed flesh of his face. Minutes ticked away and finally an official appeared to let Juan know that Bishop Zumárraga would see him now.

Don Fray Juan de Zumárraga, a priest of the Order of Saint Francis, had recently arrived as the lord of priests. He didn't normally spend his time meeting with strangers who arrived without notice but for some reason agreed to meet with Diego and greeted him with courtesy and kindness, hallmarks of his demeanor. With the bishop was an interpreter by the name of Juan González. González was quite learned and fluent in the Aztec languages, a skill he acquired while servicing the outlying missions. Juan Diego immediately fell prostrate before the bishop. Then, slowly, he lifted himself to a kneeling position. He felt very uncomfortable and a combination of fear and humility prevented Juan from looking directly at the bishop as he described his encounter with the Virgin and explained the detail of her request.

Don Fray Juan de Zumarraga, of the Order of St. Francis, was the Bishop of Mexico when Our Lady sent Juan Diego to request a chapel be built to her honor on Tepeyac Hill.

Bishop Zumárraga listened intently to Juan's story. He peppered the visitor with questions about his background, his occupation and his faith. He was impressed with Diego's sincerity and humility but had his own doubts about Juan's story of the Virgin. "My son," the bishop said, "you will have to come another time; I will calmly listen to you at another time. I still have to see, to examine carefully from the very beginning, the reason you have come, and your will and your wish."

With that, the bishop indicated Juan's dismissal. Juan rose and turned to depart, knowing that he had failed in his mission and would have to greatly disappoint his Lady. He was escorted through the hall, passing several servants who looked at him in a condescending way, and was led back out to the bitter chill of the dusty street. Disappointed with his failure, he began the long walk out of the city and back to Tepeyac hill.

The Virgin Mary Appears to Juan Diego a Second Time

Ascending the hill to its summit, Juan encountered the Lady from Heaven once again. She stood on the very spot at which he first saw her, still bathed in a supernatural radiance. Seeing Her, Juan prostrated himself and said,

Tepeyac Hill just outside of Mexico City. The site of several Marian apparitions to Juan Diego from December 9ᵗʰ – 12ᵗʰ, 1531.

"My Owner, my Matron, my Lady, the most abandoned of my Daughters, my Child, I went where you sent me to deliver your thought and your word. With great difficulty I entered the place of the lord of the priests; I saw him; before him I expressed your thought and word, just as you had ordered me. He received me well and listened carefully. But by the way he answered me, as if his heart had not accepted it, he did not believe me: 'You will have to come another time; I will calmly listen to you at another time. I still have to see, to examine carefully from the very beginning, the reason you have come, and your will and your wish.' I saw perfectly, in the way he answered me, that he thinks that possibly I am just making it up that you want a temple to be built on this site, and possibly it is not your command. Hence, I very much beg you, my Owner, my Queen, my Child, that you charge one of the more valuable nobles, a well-known person, one who is respected and esteemed, to come by and take your message and your word so that he may be believed. Because in reality I am one of those *campesinos*, a piece of rope, a small ladder, the excrement of people; I am a leaf; they order me around, lead me by force; and you, my most abandoned Daughter, my Child, my Lady, and my Queen, send me to a place where I do not belong. Forgive me, I will cause pain to your countenance and to your heart; I will displease you and fall under your wrath, my Lady, and my Owner."[69]

His words of self-loathing clearly expressed his utter disgust at his inability to deliver a positive response for his most deserving Lady.

The Virgin patiently listened to Her servant's words and replied,

"Listen my most abandoned son, know well in your heart that there are not a few of my servants and messengers to whom I could give the mandate of taking my thought and my word so that my will may be accomplished. But it is absolutely necessary that you personally go and speak about this, and that precisely through your mediation and help, my wish and my desire be realized. I beg you very much, my most abandoned son, and with all my energy I command that precisely tomorrow you go again to see the bishop. In my name you will make him know, make him listen well to my wish and desire, so that he may make my wish a reality and build my temple. And tell him once again that I personally, the Ever-Virgin Mary, the Mother of the God Téotl, am the one who is sending you there."[70]

Juan responded, "Now I take leave of you, my most abandoned Daughter, my Child, my Matron, my Lady, now you rest a bit."[71] With those words, Juan Diego returned to his home, ate dinner and retired for the evening in preparation for another long journey which would commence even before daybreak.

Sunday, December 10, 1531

While the sky was still blanketed with stars, Juan awoke and began his long trek, to the church of Santiago in Tlatelolco to answer roll call, hear Mass, and participate in a study of the faith. It was ten o'clock before Juan finally departed the church for his trip to Mexico City where he would once again attempt to meet with and convince Bishop Zumárraga of the veracity of his encounter with the Virgin Mary and of Her message for the lord of priests.

Juan Diego Meets with the Bishop a Second Time

Along the way he worried about the reaction of the bishop to the insistence of a lowly Indian on a second meeting with the church leader in just two days. Why would the bishop believe such a preposterous story, especially coming from one as undeserving as he? Juan reached out in prayer to the Blessed Virgin for the courage he would need to impose on such a busy man of God.

Juan felt very uneasy as he entered the gate to the city and approached the bishop's house. As expected, he had a great deal of difficulty convincing the bishop's servants to let him in, but after a time he succeeded in entering the patio. Like the day prior, Juan waited for hours in the cold. He paced up and down, perhaps as much to maintain warmth as to clear his head and think of the right words he might use to convince the bishop that he was telling the truth. He knew, or at least he felt, that the bishop considered him an ignorant Indian. Consequently, he knew his words needed to be chosen carefully.

Bishop Zumárraga spotted Juan and seemed annoyed at his return so soon. Still, he greeted Diego with his usual courtesy. Juan immediately knelt before the bishop and enthusiastically repeated the words of the Lady's request. Before he could fully explain, however, he broke down. Perhaps it was the lack of sleep, or possibly the toll that the long walks placed on his body. Likely it was the tension created by his feeling that, regardless of what he said or how he said it, the bishop would still not believe. He wanted so badly to please the Lady and succeed in convincing the bishop that the Virgin Mother of God wanted a temple built in her honor on Tepeyac hill. The whole experience was just too much for him.

Zumárraga gently placed his hand on Juan's shoulder in an attempt to calm him and before long, Juan regained his composure and relayed the message of the Lady in full. Naturally the bishop had a plethora of questions. "Where did you see Her? What was She like? How long did She stay?" The questioning went on for quite some time and the bishop peppered Juan with the same questions many times. But each time Diego's responses remained the same. The bishop was impressed with Juan's consistency, but still could not afford to build a church in some remote location on the word of an Indian alone. He would need something more to convince him that it was indeed the Virgin Mary who was making this request. He asked for a sign. "My patron and my lord, what is the sign that you want? [When I know, I can] go and ask the Lady from Heaven, She who sent me here."[72]

The bishop was captivated with Diego's resolve in the truth but had not thought the question through extensively. He simply told Juan to leave to the Lady the type of sign She wished to impart. With that, Juan was dismissed, all the time wondering why, at a time when the Spaniards were debating whether Indians were even fully human, the Mother of our Risen Lord was choosing him to relay a message of such importance to the bishop.

For his part, Zumárraga still had his doubts, however, and summoned a couple of his most trusted servants to follow Diego and observe where he went and to whom he spoke. They left immediately, trailing behind at a good enough distance to remain unseen yet able to track Juan's actions. They followed him to the bridge of Tepeyac where they lost sight of him in the hillside. Search as they may, they could not find him. Infuriated, they returned to the bishop's house, plotting as they did to contrive a story to cover for their own incompetence. Upon their return, they told the bishop that Diego was deceiving them and that the entire event was something of Juan's imagination. The spies agreed that if Juan showed his face at the bishop's house again, they would punish him harshly to dissuade him from lying further.

The Virgin Mary Appears to Juan Diego a Third Time

Meanwhile, Juan had climbed to the summit of Tepeyac where he was once again in the radiant presence of the Virgin Mary. "The bright aura surrounding Her enveloped him like a luminous mist, concealing his whereabouts."[73] Juan knelt at the Lady's feet and emptied his soul in sorrow. He explained that though he had done his best to convince the bishop, his story was not believed. Then he begged for a sign that the bishop requested that might convince him that Juan was telling the truth. When he finished, the Lady smiled reassuringly and in such a way as to convey her appreciation for his efforts.

> *"That is very well, my little son," the Lady said. "Return here tomorrow and you will have the sign he has requested. Then he will believe and no longer doubt or suspect you. Mark my words well, my little son: I shall richly reward you for all the worry, work and trouble you have undertaken on my behalf. You may go home now. Tomorrow, I shall be waiting here for you."*[74]

But Juan did not go straight home. He went instead to the home of his uncle Juan Bernardino. Upon entering his uncle's house, he was horrified to find the old man gravely ill. He appeared to be suffering from a rare form of salmonella known as salmonella enterica. This affliction causes high fevers, intense vomiting, and a rash. There was no cure and it generally claimed the life of its victims. It was, in fact, responsible for an epidemic that killed millions in southern Mexico.

Chapter 6
A Miraculous Day

Monday, December 11, 1531
Juan Diego Misses His Appointment with the Virgin Mary

Juan was very familiar with the symptoms of salmonella enterica and knew from his own observance that his uncle didn't have much time. He tried to comfort him as best he could and then went for the village doctor, who arrived early on Monday and applied herbal remedies. Despite the medical effort, Juan Bernardino's ailment showed no signs of improvement.

Juan was beside himself. He had promised the Lady that he would return to her on this day so that She could provide a sign for him to give to the bishop, but there was no way that Juan could leave his uncle. He agonized over the thought of disappointing the Lady but owed it to his uncle to stay with him.

By sunset it was clear that uncle Juan was dying and, short of providing some comfort, Juan Diego could do nothing to make him better. In the eyes of the Aztecs, an old man represents the tradition and the culture of an entire society. His uncle's death, therefore, would in many ways mean the end of Juan Diego's own history and a loss of his identity. He was understandably beside himself with grief.

Juan Bernardino pleaded with his nephew to go to Tlaltelolco and bring a priest to hear his confession and administer the last rites of the Catholic Church. Because of the lateness of the day, Juan promised to do so first thing in the morning.

Tuesday, December 12, 1531
Morning

In compliance with his uncle's wishes, Juan left the house at about four o'clock on Tuesday morning to begin the nine-mile journey to Tlaltelolco in the hopes of bringing a priest home to administer the sacraments to his dying uncle. As he approached the side of Mount Tepeyac, he decided to take a different road, hoping to avoid the delay of seeing the Lady, to whom he had failed to return the day prior despite his promise to Her. He instead took the road leading to the east of the hill. As he did, however, he noticed the Lady descending from the top of the hill until She rested directly in front of him, effectively blocking his passage.

> *"My most abandoned son,"* She said, *"where are you going? In what direction are you going?*
> Juan was feeling a host of emotions. He was at once embarrassed, ashamed, and fearful. If he could have run, he may have. Instead, he bowed before her and mumbled pleasantries to disguise his humiliation.
> "My Child, my most abandoned Daughter, my Lady, I hope you are happy. How did the dawn come upon

you? Does your body feel all right, my Owner and
my Child?"
Then, recovering enough to realize that he was
speaking nonsense, he said,

"I am going to give great pain to your countenance and
heart. You must know, my Child, that my uncle, a poor
servant of yours, is in his final agony; a great illness has
fallen upon him, and because of it he will die. I am in a
hurry to get to your house in Mexico; I am going to call
one of the beloved of our Lord, one of the priests, so
that he may hear his confession and prepare him. Because for this have we been born, to await the moment
of our death. But if right now I am going to do this, I
will quickly return here; I will come back to take your
thought and your word. My Matron, and my Child, forgive me, have a little patience with me; I do not want
to deceive you, my most abandoned Daughter, my
Child. Tomorrow I will come quickly."
Mary listened intently to Juan and when he had finished speaking, she said,

*"Listen and hear well in your heart, my most aban-
doned son: that which scares you and troubles you
is nothing; do not let your countenance and heart
be troubled; do not fear that sickness or any other
sickness of anxiety. Am I not here, your mother?
Are you not under my shadow and my protection?
Am I not your source of life? Are you not in the
hollow of my mantle where I cross my arms? Who
else do you need? Let nothing trouble you or cause
you sorrow. Do not worry because of your uncle's*

*sickness. He will not die of his present sickness. Be
assured in your heart that he is already healed.*"[75]

At that precise moment, Juan Bernardino was healed of his affliction. But the healing did not come without a visit by the Blessed
Virgin. The Lady, appearing to Juan Bernardino exactly as She had appeared to his nephew, told the elderly man that he had to go to Mexico
to see the bishop and reveal to him all that Bernardino had seen and the
marvelous way that the Blessed Virgin had healed him. In that way, the
bishop would name her the Ever-Virgin Holy Mary of Guadalupe.

Juan Diego didn't know the circumstances of his uncle's
healing but was greatly consoled by the Lady's words. At once his
heart became peaceful. No longer anxious for his uncle, Juan begged
the Lady to give him the sign that he could immediately take to the
bishop. The compliant Lady said,

*"Go up, my most abandoned son, to the top of the
hill, and there, where you saw me and I gave you my
instructions, there you will see many diverse flowers:
cut them, gather them, put them together. Then come
down here and bring them before me."*

Juan climbed to the top of the hill to the exact spot where the
Virgin had appeared prior. He was surprised to find exquisite flowers
from Castile in full bloom at a time of the year in which ice hardens
upon the earth. In fact, the hilltop was not a conducive area for such
flowers even in the summer months. "It was covered with rocks, thistles, thorns, cacti, mesquites; and if small herbs grew there, during the
month of December, they were all eaten up and wilted by the ice."[76]
Juan was taken by the smell of their fragrance and noticed that the
blooms were filled with the morning dew.

Without a thought, he cut and gathered the blossoms as instructed. He formed a hollow with his tilma and placed them there in

order to transport them with greater ease. With haste he descended the hill and returned to the Queen of Heaven as he had been instructed. Upon seeing the cut flowers, the Virgin "took them in Her small hands; and then She placed them in the hollow of his mantle"[77] telling Juan,

> *"My most abandoned son, these different flowers are proof, the sign, that you will take to the bishop. In My name tell him that he is to see in them what I want, and with this he should carry out my wish and my will. And you, you are my ambassador; in you I place all my trust. With all my strength I command you that only in the presence of the bishop are you to open your mantle and let him know and reveal to him what you are carrying. You will recount everything well; you will tell him how I sent you to climb to the top of the hill to go cut flowers, and all that you saw and admired. With this you will change the heart of the lord of the priests so that he will do his part to build and erect my temple that I have asked him for."*[78]

Juan hurried off immediately. Following the road to Mexico, he was exceedingly happy. He knew that now, with the proof the bishop had requested, he would believe that Juan had indeed been visited by the Queen of Peace. Her words swirled in his head. *"And you, you are my ambassador; in you I place all my trust."* Such an incredible statement! Juan knew the harsh truth. Indians were considered to be unworthy of any trust, a people who imagined things and easily lied and hence a people who should be dominated and punished. But his Heavenly Visitor had changed all that. She was revealing an ultimate truth about the Indians: they are the most trusted ambassadors of heaven. Those once considered to be unworthy of ordination by church regulation, were to be the most trusted ambassadors, the chosen spokepersons of God. What's more, She, the Mother of the Risen Lord, even had the complexion of an Indian.

As soon as he arrived at the house, Juan ran into the doorkeepers and servants of the lord of priests and begged them to tell the bishop that he needed to see him, but none would do so. It was still night and the servants knew that the bishop was not one to be disturbed at night. Despite Juan's jubilance at the Lady's words of reassurance, he was again forced to wait a very long time, rendering him of little to no importance in the eyes of the bishop. When the servants noticed that Juan carried something in his mantle, however, they approached him demanding to see what he carried. Realizing that they intended him harm had they not gotten their way Juan allowed them to see just a bit of the flowers. Immediately the staff recognized that he carried blossoming flowers that could not be obtained at this time of year and they were astonished. Three different times they tried to take some of the flowers from his mantle, but they were unable to do it because each time they grabbed at a flower, it became part of the fabric of the tilma. That is when they decided it was time to summon the bishop.

Upon being informed of Juan's presence, the bishop anticipated that this despicable Indian might carry the proof he had requested and ordered that he be brought before him. The servants immediately went to get him and led him to bishop Zumárraga. Juan entered the room, taking stock of who was present. Standing next to the Bishop were Juan Gonzales and Bishop Sebastián Ramírez de Fuenleal, the Bishop of Santo Domingo. There were others present too, some of the bishops' servants perhaps. Diego "knelt before the bishop as he had done before and once again, he told him everything he had seen and admired and also Her message."[79]

> *"My owner and my lord, I have accomplished what you asked for; I went to tell my Matron, my Owner, the Lady from Heaven, Holy Mary, the precious Mother of God Téotl, how you had asked me for a sign in order to*

believe me, so that you might build Her temple where She is asking you to erect it. And besides, I told Her that I had given you my word that I would bring you a sign and a proof of Her will that you want to receive from my hands. When She received your thought and your word, She accepted willingly what you asked for, a sign and a proof so that Her desire and will may come about. And today when it was still night, She sent me to come and see you once again. But I asked Her for the sign and the proof of Her will that you asked me for and that She had agreed to give to me. Immediately She complied. She sent me to the top of the hill where I had seen Her before, so that there I might cut the flowers from Castile. After I had cut them, I took them to the bottom of the hill. And She, with Her precious little hands, took them; She arranged them in the hollow of my mantle, so that I might bring them to you, and deliver them to you personally. Even though I knew well that the top of the hill was not a place where flowers grow, that only stones, thistles, thorns, cacti and mesquites abound there, I still was neither surprised nor doubted. As I was arriving at the top of the hill, my eyes became fixed: It was the Flowering Earth! It was covered with all kinds of flowers from Castile, full of dew and shining brilliantly. Immediately I went to cut them. And She told me why I had to deliver them to you: so that you might see the sign you requested and so that you will believe in Her will; and also so that the truth of my word and my message might be manifested. Here they are. Please receive them."[80]

When he finished speaking, Juan opened his white tilma in which the flowers were gathered and arranged by Mary's hand. At

Juan Diego unfurles his tilma to release the colorful flowers that he collected at the behest of the Blessed Virgin. He is unaware that the Mother of God also "painted" a portrait, a miraculous image, on the tilma.

that moment the multi-colored blooms fell to the ground. Immediately the bishop and his servants fell to their knees. It was not so much the sight of the flowers that caused their exacerbation, however. It was the sight of something of which Juan himself had no knowledge. It was a portrait of the Virgin Mary exactly as She had appeared to Juan. A self-portrait painted by the Mother of God when she reached into Juan's tilma to rearrange the flowers. The astonished look that coated the faces of the bishop and his servants as they stared, not at the flowers, but at Juan's mantle, caused Juan to look down at his own tilma. He too was overcome with emotion.

The bishop's conversion was instantaneous. Tears filled his eyes and sadness filled his heart as he prayed to the Blessed Virgin Mary begging "Her to forgive him for not having believed Her will, Her heart and Her word."[81] He reached for Juan and carefully "untied the tilma at the back of Juan's neck and reverently conveyed the transfigured garment to his private oratory where he could contemplate it to his heart's content."[82] Finally able to compose himself, the bishop asked Juan to remain at his home for another day.

Wednesday, December 13, 1531
Morning

Early on the morning of December 13, the bishop began making arrangements for the construction of the temple. He had overnight decided to have a small chapel built immediately while waiting for plans to be drafted for the construction of a larger, more elaborate temple.

Word of the great sign given by the Virgin Mary had already begun to spread throughout the village and all who heard the story were deeply moved. For his part, the bishop processed the tilma through the village to the cathedral accompanied by multitudes who followed in joyous prayer.

Mid-day

After leaving the cathedral, the bishop asked Juan to take him to the very spot on Tepeyac hill on which the Lady wanted Her hermitage built. Juan obliged and when satisfied that the bishop knew the exact location of the Lady's apparitions, he asked permission to depart for the village of Tolpetlac. He very much wanted to visit his uncle whom he had not seen since the old man had been at death's door. Juan certainly trusted that the Lady had cured his uncle as promised, but longed to see him restored to good health. Rather than letting him leave alone, the bishop told his men to accompany Juan, who had now been elevated to a "royal" status, to his uncle's house in proper escort.

When they arrived, they found Juan Bernardino healthy, albeit surprised to see his nephew in the company of the bishop's honor guard. A crowd of villagers joined them, and Diego explained how, while traveling to Tlaltelolco to get a priest, he was intercepted at Tepeyac hill by the Queen of Heaven who told him that his uncle was healed and no longer in need of a priest.

That is when Juan Bernardino confirmed to Juan Diego and the others that he was in fact healed by the Virgin Mary and that She appeared to him personally to enact the healing. He described Her appearance which matched exactly the verbal description given by Juan Diego and the portrait appearing on his tilma. Further, Bernardino noted that the Mother of God also told him that he had to go to Mexico to see the bishop. Finally, he told them the name by which the Virgin Mary wished that Her precious image be called. The interpreter strained to hear and understand Juan Bernardino's words which, to him, sounded like, "the Ever-Virgin Holy Mary of Guadalupe."*[83] To Juan Diego and all the Aztec people, "it was highly significant that Our Lady had revealed her name to Juan Bernardino and not to his nephew, because for them an elderly person was a bearer, a keeper, of ancient culture. Tradition legitimized his authority."[84]

The bishop's men had seen great things already, but the healing and appearance of Our Lady to Diego's uncle was another miracle that could not be ignored. They told Juan Bernardino that they wanted to take him to the bishop so that he might explain personally all that he had just relayed.

Thursday, December 14, 1531

Juan Diego, his uncle and the bishop's men departed for Mexico City where they retold every detail of the story to the bishop.

* NOTE: Juan Bernardino could not have used the name Guadalupe since the alphabet of his native language of Nahuatl does not include the letters G and D. He must have noted a similar name which the interpreter heard as Guadalupe. History and Ethnography, determined that the Virgin actually used the word Coatlaxopeuh, which means "she who breaks, stamps or crushes the serpent." This too is the equivalent of the Immaculate Conception. This study was corroborated by two independent authorities in 1936 and 1953.(See endnote on page 185 for more information.)

"Zumárraga was astounded, for the name Guadalupe had no connection whatever with Mexico but was the name of a famous Marian shrine in distant Spain"[85] that had existed in the eastern province of Estremadura for centuries. He knew, therefore, that the identity had to be a mistake, but none the less marveled at the fact that Our Lady would have chosen Nahuatl words so similar to the Spanish translation as to be mistaken for the name Guadalupe.

This was no accident. It was Our Lady's way of appealing to both the Spaniards and the Indians. "When the Spanish heard the name Guadalupe, they immediately associated it with their shrine. They understood from this that She was not the exclusive property of the Aztecs."[86]

Zumárraga's mind surely drifted to the little-known statue of the Immaculate Conception, which was kept in the choir of the Spanish shrine. "The image of Our Lady of Guadalupe in Estremadura is a statue of the Madonna with Child, said to have been carved by St. Luke."[87] It very much resembled the sacred image which Mary imprinted on Juan Diego's tilma.

The small statue itself has a miraculous history. The Catholic tradition explains that the statue was given by Pope St. Gregory the Great (590 – 604) to St. Leander, Bishop of Seville. In the year 711, when the Muslims overtook most of the Spanish peninsula, they imposed their own religion in all territories now under their domination. By 719, they had defeated the last of the Visigoth kings of Spain, expanding the Muslim territory to the Pyrenees mountains. The retreating Christians, however, managed to keep the statue carved by St. Luke in their possession, carrying it to the mountains of Asturias. "Threatened with annihilation, they placed the statue in an iron casket and buried it in an unmarked place in the province of Extremadura, where it remained hidden for many centuries."[88] Then, sometime in the mid-thirteenth century, the Blessed Mother appeared to a man named Gil who tended his herd. She instructed him to dig in a very specific place where he would find Her statue.

She also told him to have a chapel built on that spot where She could be venerated. Gil notified ecclesiastical authorities of the apparition. They came to the village of Guadalupe and dug up the casket on the exact spot in which Mary had instructed Gil to dig. In the casket was the statue of Our Lady and a note confirming its identity. In accordance with Our Lady's instructions, a small chapel was built and then a larger one. By 1340, kings of Spain were coming to the shrine in thanksgiving for their victories over the Muslims. A monastery under the care of the Hermits of St. Jerome was built on the site in later years. This is the very site visited by Queen Isabella, King Ferdinand, Christopher Columbus, and Hernán Cortés, all devout Catholics. Bishop Zumárraga also prayed and worshipped at this site.

Regardless of the name by which Our Lady would be called, the miracles, it seemed to the bishop, just kept on coming. The bishop invited Juan and his uncle to stay at his house where they would be honored guests for the next two weeks.

The word was also spreading furiously among the native population and "thousands were flocking to the cathedral to see for themselves "the Mother of the white man's God."[89] For those who made the journey, the experience was transcendent. The image they viewed on the tilma was of a young girl with beautifully delicate features, an olive complexion, rosy cheeks, and long brown hair. Her face, with eyes looking down, projected humility and at the same time gave the impression that She was alive.

Her clothes were equally beautiful. "She wore a rose-colored garment overlaid with a fine lace-like sheath worked with an exquisite floral design of gold. A star-studded, greenish-blue mantle covered her head and fell to her feet."[90] An aura of sunlight surrounded the figure, magnifying the intensity of Her beauty such as no description can adequately portray. It was abundantly clear to all whose eyes gazed upon Her likeness that "no one on earth had painted Her precious image."

Perhaps the most astounding feature about the image, they discerned, is that the detail is sharper when viewing it from a

The original image of Our Lady of Guadalupe as She "painted" it on the tilma of Juan Diego at 6:45 in the morning of December 12, 1531. This image is displayed in the Basilica of Our Lady of Guadalupe in Mexico City, Mexico.

distance than when standing up close. Normally, it is just the opposite, but viewers of the tilma noticed that they could "scarcely see the stars in Her robe; yet they are dazzling from a distance. And from [near], her robe is not the greenish-blue one sees from a distance, but a much bluer and darkish blue. The pink of her gown is very pale close-up, but very rosy at some distance."[91] Conversely Her face is clearer in detail when viewed close-up but is veiled in shadow when viewed from a distance.

It wasn't the brilliance of her clothes, however, that made the miraculous image of the Mother of God so endearing to the natives of Mexico. It wasn't even the stars on Her robe or the humble expression on Her face. It was rather that the image assumed the look of a Mexican when viewed by a native. The Mother of God was indeed one of them!

Chapter 7
Our Lady's Request Becomes a Reality

Friday, December 15, 1531

With the tilma safely displayed at the cathedral, Bishop Zumárraga contemplated compliance with Mary's request for a suitable temple at Tepeyac hill but felt the urgency to build something immediately as numerous pilgrims had already begun ascending the hill daily to pray at the site of Her apparitions. So many Mexicans and Spaniards responded to his call for volunteers that construction of a small stone chapel, or hermitage, was completed in less than two weeks' time. It contained a single room approximately fifteen feet by fifteen feet.

After witnessing the miraculous image on Diego's tilma, Bishop Zumarraga agreed to build the church that Our Lady requested. Zumarraga ordered the immediate construction of a small church which was eventually replaced with this larger church.

Tuesday, December 26, 1531

With the hermitage complete, a jubilant procession transported the sacred image from the cathedral to Tepeyac for placement at its new home. Winding along city streets, crowds of excited people followed Franciscan and Dominican missionaries all led by the bishop. Hundreds, perhaps thousands, lined the streets and boats, decorated to acknowledge the glory of the moment, anchored along both sides of Lake Texcoco which was split by the causeway.

The jubilation spilled into the streets as observers danced to joyous music and threw flowers of adoration while singing "'the Virgin is one of us! Our Immaculate Mother! Our Sovereign Lady is one of us!'"[92]

The Celebration Turns Deadly
Prompting the First Miracle Associated with the Image

As the front of the procession stretched inside the hermitage, Bishop Zumárraga enshrined the tilma. While outside, the celebration began to get a bit out of control. One group of excited Mexicans caught up in the jubilation, "shot volleys of arrows into the air, and one of these shafts struck a spectator in the neck, killing him instantly."[93] Some from the crowd lifted the man's limp body and quickly weaved through throngs of onlookers as they carried him to the hermitage. Placing the body in front of Our Lady's image, they prayed fervently for a miracle. A large crowd of people pressed in as their voices were raised in petition for Mary's intervention. "Minutes later, the dead man opened his eyes and rose to his feet fully recovered."[94]

Audible gasps could be heard as the man stood. These were followed by a paroxysm of cheers of jubilation as many in the diverse crowd of Spaniards and Mexicans hugged and danced with delight. As word of the miracle at the hermitage spread along the parade route and throughout the region, any hostilities that had besmeared the relations between the two races began to subside.

Evening

By the day's end many in the jubilant crowd had left and the streets were returning to their previous day's norm. Bishop Zumárraga needed to depart Mexico for Spain, where he would remain for an extended time, but didn't feel comfortable leaving without first securing someone to maintain the new chapel. He could think of no one better than the very person who carried Mary's message to him. Turning to Juan Diego the bishop asked if he would take charge of the new hermitage. Knowing that his life now belonged to the Lady,

Juan accepted the bishop's offer with great humility and appreciation.

Juan would not be alone in his new charge. The man who was raised to life before the miraculous image also devoted the remainder of his life to Our Lady, working as a custodian in the hermitage ensuring that it was clean each day following visits by hundreds of pilgrims.

Chapter 8
All the Remaining Days
Wednesday, December 27, 1531 to
December 31, 1543

Over the ensuing weeks, Juan Diego gave his property in Tolpetlac to his beloved uncle and helped add a room to the chapel. He would spend the rest of his life in devotion to Our Lady, propagating the story of the apparitions while explaining the significance of the events to the hundreds of pilgrims that visited the small temple in "an ever-growing tide of devotion."[95] He carefully noted to each visitor the significance of Our Lady's appearance at the site of a former Pagan temple honoring the mother-goddess Tonantzin, a temple that Cortés had destroyed. The site, he noted, was carefully chosen by Our Mother to reinforce the fact that Christianity was to replace the Aztec religion. So impactful was his testimony that Mexicans began to refer to the "sacred image as a picture of *Tonantzin* ('Our Mother') or *Teo-nantzin* ('God's Mother')."[96]

The story of Juan Diego, the Apparitions of Our Lady, and the miracle restoring life to the dead became common knowledge everywhere. Artisans painted copies of the miraculous image and packaged them with codices of the story which they circulated throughout Mexico by the thousands. This resulted in a great number of conversions.

For native Mexicans, however, hearing the story from a fellow Mexican who spoke the native language and also happened to be a Christian, was a powerful experience. In repeating the story of the apparitions thousands of times, reciting the words Our Lady had spoken to him, and showing the image on the tilma, Juan was responsible for the conversion of hundreds of thousands of Mexicans to Christianity. The Catholic faith spread exponentially throughout Mexico well beyond the bounds of the Aztec empire.

The missionaries were overwhelmed with the throngs who sought them out for instruction in the faith and Baptism. As many as six thousand were Baptized in a single day. One of those missionaries, Fr. Toribio Motolinía, recorded:

> "Had I not witnessed it with my own eyes, I should not venture to report it. I have to affirm that at the convent of Quecholac, another priest and myself baptized 14,200 souls in five days. We even imposed the Oil of Catechumens and the Holy Chrism on all of them – an undertaking of no little labor."[97]

It is estimated that between 8,000,000 and 9,000,000 Aztec people converted to Catholicism over the next eight to ten years, numbers unprecedented in the history of Christianity. Dr. Ibarra of Chilapa noted,

"...The Catholic Faith spread with the rapidity of light from the rising sun, through the wide extent and beyond the bounds of the ancient empire of Mexico. Innumerable multitudes from every tribe, every district, every race, in this immense country...who were grossly superstitious, who were ruled by the instincts of cruelty, oppressed by every form of violence, and utterly degraded, returned upon themselves at the credible announcement of the admirably portentous apparition of Our Lady of Guadalupe; recognized their natural dignity; forgot their misfortunes; put off their instinctive ferocity; and, unable to resist such sweet and tender invitations, came in crowds to cast their grateful hearts at the feet of so loving a Mother, and to mingle their tears of emotion with the regenerating waters of Baptism."[98]

Indeed, missionaries could scarcely enter a town where throngs of villagers would not run into the streets to greet them requesting the Rite of Baptism. Others fell to their knees, pleading for the immediate administration of the sacrament. Most prominent historians of the time credited the conversions to the apparitions of Our Lady to Juan Diego.

To accommodate the large influx of Catholics, "churches, monasteries, convents, hospitals, schools and workshops sprang up all over the country in the wake of this phenomenal missionary conquest."[99] Before long, Mexico would become a beacon of the Catholic Faith, sending missionaries into Florida, California and Japan.

Juan Diego, meanwhile, continued his custody of the small chapel. He installed the Sacred image on his tilma over the tiny altar, a place of peaceful and reflective prayer for Juan. He continued to live a life of humility and austerity and, in a practice most unusual for the times, was granted special permission by the bishop to receive the Holy Eucharist as many as three times per week. Juan constantly occupied himself with the affairs of God so that most that knew him, particularly the Indians, "revered [him] as a man of great culture and lofty thinking, as befits a man who led such a holy life."[100]

The Aztec converts frequently sought his advice and asked for his intervention with the Blessed Virgin. They called him *pilgrim* because he could frequently be seen attending service and devotions by himself and was often found to be repentant and performing many propitiations.

Between January 1, 1544 and May 30, 1548

Life over the ensuing years continued pretty much unabated for Juan Diego as he persisted in his position of authority over the little chapel of Tepeyac hill. Mexico, however, had undergone some significant changes punctuated by the "Second Audience headed by Bishop Sebastián Ramírez y Fuenleal. Exploitation of the Mexicans by the Spanish soldiers became increasingly infrequent as the two races gradually intermarried and settled down together in religious and social harmony. The Bishop's rule was followed by the wise administration of the Marques de Mendoza, the first Viceroy, and then by a long line of Viceroys and Archbishops who were to give the country nearly two hundred years of political and economic stability and peace."[101]

While the bishop, and now most of the people in central Mexico, knew the exact spot on which the Blessed Mother appeared to Juan Diego on Tepeyac hill, the place of her fourth and final apparition to Juan in 1531 had been largely ignored. That changed when Bishop Zumárraga asked Juan to show him the exact spot at which Mary intercepted him as he hurried off to fetch a priest to deliver the final rites of the church to his dying uncle. Juan was happy to oblige, but upon reaching the vicinity of the apparition, he hesitated, unsure of the exact spot. At that moment, "a spring suddenly gushed forth from the ground a short distance away. Juan remembered that it was on this exact spot that She had spoken to him and asked him to climb the hill to gather flowers for the Bishop."[102] The spring water was, and remains to this day, very clean but with an unpleasant acetic taste and a slight odor.

Naturally, all that witnessed the advent of the spring thought it a miraculous sign from the Blessed Virgin and many were cured of various ailments and diseases as a result of drinking the water or anointing themselves with it. The practice continued, and three centuries later, French antiquarian Eugene Boban, a noted archaeologist and member of the French Scientific Commission in Mexico, a man known for basing his opinions and actions on reason and knowledge rather than on religious belief or emotional response, noted:

> *"The spring [of Guadalupe] is to be found in the center of a little chapel of very interesting Moorish style. A crowd, armed with vases and bottles of every size and shape, were gathered around in order to draw this miraculous water at its source, just like Lourdes water, and they take it to cure all illnesses."*[103]

In 1544, Juan Diego's uncle Juan Bernardino passed away at the age of eighty-six but not before being visited by the Blessed Virgin one more time on his last day on earth. Bishop Zumárraga arranged for him to be interned under the hermitage and his home was converted to a chapel.

Shortly after the start of the year 1548, Bishop Zumárraga was named the first Archbishop of the New World. In his new capacity he undertook an arduous journey to Tepetlaoztoc and baptized, confirmed, and married about fourteen thousand Mexicans. The travel and the arduous schedule took a toll on his health, however, and by the time he returned to Mexico City toward the end of

May, he fell seriously ill. It was while he lay on his deathbed that servants brought him word that Cortés had died in Seville on December 2, 1547. They also conveyed the dreadful news of the untimely passing of Juan Diego.

On May 30, 1548, just four years following the passing of his beloved uncle, seventy-four-year-old Juan Diego breathed his last in the presence of The Blessed Virgin Mary, who came to console him at the hour of his death. Juan's bedroom at Tepeyac hill was converted to a baptistry and a tablet noting the Indian's station in life was placed on the wall. It reads:

> *"In this place, Our Lady of Guadalupe appeared to*
> *an Indian named Juan Diego who is buried in this*
> *church."*[104]

Three days later, and just one month after accepting the title of Archbishop conferred upon him by Pope Paul III, Bishop Don Fray Juan de Zumárraga also entered into his eternity. In his last letter, Zumárraga noted how happy he was having just confirmed some four thousand Indians during the past few days.

All four men left this earth without benefit of seeing the grand temple constructed at Tepeyac, though none had doubted its eventual construction would become reality. Now each was in the presence of Our Lady of Tepeyac and Her Son, the True and Living God.

Zumárraga was succeeded by Dominican Friar Alonso de Montúfar who, like Zumárraga, was a great devotee of Our Lady of Guadalupe. His position, however, was in "conflict with the Franciscans, for they were very suspicious of the apparitions"[105] as they believed that the "cult" created by Juan Diego was really a secret devotion to Tonantzin, a pagan goddess whose temple once stood on Tepeyac Hill. Emotions ran so high that an inquiry was needed to sort out the facts from the fiction. In the end, no evidence could be presented to substantiate the claims of idolatry. In fact, during the inquiry, testimony acknowledged that "the whole population deeply revered the image of Our Lady from the very beginning. Indians from all social classes made pilgrimages to it. Some were so zealous in revering the image that the monks had to restrain them."[106] The "cult" was very much alive even a quarter-century after the apparitions had occurred.

Part III

Conversions Resulting from Image of the Mother of God

From the time of their arrival in Mexico in 1517 to the time of the Marian apparitions to Juan Diego in 1531, the dearth of missionaries from the Franciscan and Dominican orders were able to convert only a few hundred thousand Aztec Indians to Christianity. The conversion process met with great resistance. It was difficult, time consuming, and not without bloodshed. While that effort was moderately successful, it was clear that the missionaries alone would not be able to convert Mexico, especially at a time when the Protestant Reformation was claiming hundreds of thousands of Catholics in Europe.

Incredibly, in the ten-year period following Her apparitions, the total number of Aztecs converted climbed to over nine million, and all of those converted post-apparition were voluntary conversions accomplished peacefully and without bloodshed. While Cortés and his men captured Indian territory for the Spanish Crown, "Our Lady captured the hearts of the native people...for faith."[107]

For a deeper understanding of the impact of Mary's apparitions to the Aztec Indian people, and the subsequent spiritual conquest of Mexico, it is necessary to delve into the miraculous nature of the apparitions themselves as well as into the precious image that the Queen of Heaven "painted" on Juan Diego's tilma. "The image was comprehensible to the indigenous people of Mexico, a clear pictorial message...[and] in 1945, [it was] confirmed that the symbols in the image match those of an ancient Aztec language, Amoxtli."[108] The miracles associated with these two events underscore the many ways in which the Mother of God addressed the Nahuatl-speaking population, evoking emotions that had been absent in them since the 1519 fall of Moctezuma.

Chapter 9
The Precise Language of Our Lady as a Means of Conversion

It should be noted first that Mary spoke to Juan Diego using imagery known only to the Aztec natives, and Her revelations consist of three parts: a request, a promise, and an affirmation. First, Mary *requests* that Juan tell the bishop to build a temple on Tepeyac hill. Second, She *promises* to give something to the people in this temple. Finally, the Mother of God explains, using a series of words in accordance with Mexican custom, exactly what it is that She will give to the Aztec people. Essentially, Her promises to the native Mexicans include, *"My love; My compassion; My help; and My protection."*[109]

These "maternal" acts impart to Juan Her promise to actually *be* the universal mother, and those promises are affirmed with the emphatic proclamation, *"I am your merciful Mother."* Just as the crucified Christ symbolically chose St. John the Apostle, who was standing with Mary at the foot of Jesus' cross, to represent all humanity when He said "John, behold your Mother," so too, Mary chooses Juan Diego to represent all Mexican natives in the inclusion of Her maternity.

The Holy Mother also establishes a series of conditions under which the natives may enjoy Her motherhood, conditions that are based upon traditional Christian norms: The native Mexicans must love Her; they must cry to Her, they must seek Her, and they must have confidence in Her. These conditions contain the textbook means for man to show appreciation for Mary and the perfect way for a mother to express Her love for Her children.

From the very essence of Her language, the Nahuatl speaking people were comfortable in the knowledge that Mary is not only the Mother of God, but their own Mother, and as such "truly helps and shows compassion to all who love Her, as if they were under Her shadow and under Her protection..."[110]

The precise words that Mary used when speaking to Juan Diego could not alone adequately explain the non-violent, deliberate conversion of so many Aztecs in such a short period of time. There had to be more and clearly there was. The extraordinary image left on Juan Diego's tilma "turned out to be a strong impetus for the birth of a new nation, of two ethnic groups and two cultures: Spanish and Indian. The Image is so closely connected with the history of Mexico that it is unimaginable without it."[111]

Chapter 10
Mary's Use of the Tilma
as a Means of Conversion

Juan Diego did not know when he left the presence of the Mother of God on that chilly Tuesday morning in December 1531 that She had fashioned an impression of Her own image on the inside of his tilma. Nor was he the first to be made aware that the image had appeared. That privilege belonged to the bishop of Mexico City, who subsequently carried the image in solemn procession and displayed it at jubilant celebrations. But not even the bishop "could have imagined the awe the image would evoke in the natives, for he had no idea that it encoded a message, which would bring about the conversion of nine million Indians to Christianity in just eight years."[112] For the Aztecs, it was not only about how the image appeared on Juan Diego's tilma, but what the depiction represented, that was so miraculous.

After hearing the story or seeing the tilma, it was not only individuals or whole families, but rather entire tribes that were rushing into the monasteries to request Baptism of the Franciscan and Dominican missionaries. They came from distant villages, including places where no evangelist had ever visited. The missionaries were bewildered and confused. Why the sudden rush to convert?

The Image of Our Lady of Guadalupe on the tilma was no insignificant manifestation to the Indian people. Tilmas were used by Indians to carry their newborn children to the temples to be dedicated to a god. During ceremonies of marriage, an Indian woman's huipilli, or shirt, and a man's tilma, were tied together signifying the couple's mutual bond. To the Indian natives, Mary's use of the tilma signified "a mystical marriage between Our Lady and the Mexican people. It signified giving up former idols and entering a new covenant with God."[113] Tilmas were also worn for protection from the sun and the cold, indicating that Mary would safeguard them in times of trouble. They were used to carry food, equating Mary to the "bearer of lifegiving food in the personage of Her Son, Jesus Christ. In short, by using the tilma to transmit Her sacred image to the Indian people, Mary 'proclaimed the Gospel in a manner that was rooted in Indian culture.'"[114]

Chapter 11
What Our Lady's Image on the Tilma Represents to the Aztecs

The native Indians of Mesoamerica worshipped many gods, but the connection between them and the gods was unidimensional, devoid of any type of personal relationship. Mary, by contrast, engaged the Aztecs with association through the many symbols identified on the miraculous cloth. Every aspect of Her image presented a symbolic meaning understood by the Aztec people. Unlike the polytheistic gods, the woman in the image was unmasked, showing the native population that She possesses human qualities. Despite the humanity, however, Mary projects herself as a powerful Queen. Symbolic of Her power, She stands on the moon and covers the sun. She wears a bluish-green mantle, a color the Aztecs reserved for royalty. Yet, "She is surrounded by clouds and mist which point to

Her divine origin and mission. Hence She came with a message from another world."[115]

The hair on the woman in the image is long and flowing, a symbol of virginity in the Aztec culture, and she has a black sash tied with a bow around her waist indicating that the woman is pregnant. The quincunx flower over her womb symbolizes divinity and transcendence. Even this five-part flower, which has four components that meet in the center, holds significant meaning to the Aztecs as it represents their "ideal of harmony and beauty, while the number five symbolized man meeting God."[116] Though these various symbols were generally meaningless to the Spanish, the image imparted the clear message to the native Indians of the time. Simply stated, the "Lady in the image is a virgin, who bears the true God in Her womb. To the Indians, who used pictograms on a daily basis, it was a perfectly intelligible code."[117]

Beneath the crescent moon (a symbol the Spanish believed to be an allusion to the Woman noted by St. John in the Book of Revelations) on which the Mother of God stands is an angel who appears to be supporting the entirety of its weight. The angel holds the Queen's blue, star-laden mantle in his right hand, and Her tunic in his left. Each contains a variety of symbols, which though meaningless to the Spaniards, were quite evocative to the Aztecs. The mantle and the stars symbolize the sky, while the flowers on Her tunic symbolize the earth. To the native Indians, the color blue itself signified heaven, the very place of the gods. To the priestly class, the map of stars on the mantle held a clearer and more consequential message. That is, "the true God, Lord of the universe, was in the woman's womb, and knowledge of this [fact] was being communicated from the other world."

Transmitting a message that both the natives and the upper castes could understand clearly hastened the course of conversion for the Aztecs. It also gave rise to conversions among their adjacent tribes, people of the entire region of Latin America, and even populations on other continents, where fear of the potential loss of influence among members of the higher castes was soon forgotten.

The Spanish people knew little or nothing of the Aztec imagery but interpreted the image on the tilma as a Christian icon projecting symbols which they claimed as their own. As noted by Gazegorz Gorney and Janusz Rosikon, authors of *Guadalupe Mysteries: Deciphering the Code*, the color blue on "the mantle symbolizes immortality and eternal happiness with God in heaven." The sash around Her waist symbolized "virginity, purity, and devotion to God." The "cloud surrounding Mary signifies the invisible and inexpressible God [while] the pink color of the tunic recalls the red of self-sacrificing love. The leaves on the tunic are a symbol of paradise. The moon under Our Lady's feet is an allusion to the woman in the Apocalypse. The ermine lining of Mary's tunic signifies Her royalty and purity and the stars on the mantle indicate Her title of Queen of Heaven." In addition, the gold brooch has a cross, the most important of Christian symbols. The Angel is Mary's servant. [Her] hands folded in prayer show honor, praise and worship to God [while] Mary's inwardly turned eyes symbolize contemplation and spiritual union with God. Mary's bent knee signifies Her humility before God and [Her] smile expresses joy in being in the presence of the Creator."[118]

It was not only the appearance of the image on the tilma and the symbols attributed to the image that kindled the faith among the natives. There were also miracles associated with the image. In 1545, an epidemic broke out in and near the capital city. With no natural immunity to the infectious disease, the epidemic claimed the lives of some twelve thousand natives over the course of several months. Just when it seemed there was no end in sight, the "Franciscans organized a children's procession to the image of Our Lady of Guadalupe to beg for help. Shortly after, the epidemic died out; this was universally attributed to the intervention of Our Lady."[119]

The miraculous image on the tilma of Juan Diego synthesized two cultures. It brought together the Spanish and the Indian civilizations, societies and ethnicities, creating from them a single race of Mexican people. On the tilma, Mary appears as dark-skinned and when viewed from a distance She takes on the appearance of an Indian. However, when viewed from up close, She looks like a white woman.

The image's contrast in skin tone caused the two races to renounce their desire for retribution and resolve to surmount their mutual abhorrence. Appearing as a Mestizo, Mary overcame the hatred with a natural blending to the two races. For the first time since the conquest of Mesoamerica, the Mestizos were viewed in an entirely different light, and the curse that was once manifested in a homeless, rejected child suddenly became a blessing. "So, the present Mexico arose when She told Juan Diego that She was proud of being a compassionate Mother, both to him as well as to all the inhabitants of Mexico. She added that Her Motherhood extends to all those who love Her, trust Her, and call upon Her name. That won the hearts of Indians."[120] Thus, after the violent and bloody conquest of Mesoamerica by Hernán Cortés, its inculturation was peaceful and swift, but only because Our Lady of Guadalupe was its impetus.

Part IV

More Revelations from the Image of the Mother of God

The miraculous image of the Queen of Heaven on Juan Diego's tilma has been the object of investigation for five centuries, beginning with the first analysis being performed by a group of physicians and painters in the year 1633 and culminating with the most recent study of record performed by a Mexican engineer in 2006. Along with the Shroud of Turin, Juan Diego's tilma may well be the most studied cloth in world history. The studies of the fabric have been conducted by physicians, painters, mathematicians, photographers, chemists, ophthalmologists, opticians, biophysicists, engineers, astronomers, musicians, priests. and historians. Some of these professionals shared the Catholic faith while others did not. Some were believers and still others, skeptics. Yet all seem to share the conclusion that the image on the cloth could not have been made by human hands and is thus extra-scientific. That is to say that the appearance of the image on the tilma is without scientific explanation and consequently must be of heavenly origin.

The following chapters will review and summarize the many investigations and studies of the image of Our Lady of Guadalupe on the tilma of Juan Diego and explore the information and discoveries retrieved from each of these studies, both scientific and intuitive. They will also show the evolution of thought as each new advancement in science and in medicine enabled researchers to examine the cloth and the image microscopically and using various forms of light,

Chapter 12
Seventeenth Century Investigations of the Tilma

1648 to 1666

On March 13, 1666, a group of physicians and painters performed the first known scientific analysis of the image of Our Lady of Guadalupe on the tilma of Juan Diego. Seven master painters were assigned the task of examining the cloth to determine if the image had been painted by human hands. One of the painters was a cleric and the inspection took place in the presence of the Viceroy and other dignitaries.

After a thorough examination, the painters testified that "it is impossible for any man to paint such a well-formed image on that rough cloth. They praised the elegance of the image, the beauty of the face and hands, the colors and gold stars."[121]

The painters could not, however, decide if the painting was oil or tempera. It seemed to the men to have the appearance of both, yet they knew from touching the cloth that it would have been impossible to paint on it regardless of the type of paint used. That was not the only anomaly they discovered. When the cloth was inspected from the reverse, the image could be seen in its entirety without losing any sharpness to the image or brightness of the colors. This was a clear indication that no sizing was used making it more impossible to paint on such a coarse cloth. The study was brief, but the final report, signed by Professor Becerra Tanco, drew a great deal of attention to the diffraction effect on the material.

The professor also addressed the fabric of the tilma, explaining that "the rough cloth is made of a palm thread called iczotl, which is softer than other kinds of maguey. He explained that there are three kinds of maguey, one of which was used by the poor Indians for their tilmas or cloaks. These cloths are also called ayate, just like the coarser maguey fabrics used for sackcloth."[122] He pointed out that though the tilma had undergone some corruption, the colors of the likeness are still brilliant. Men with no particular expertise, but who had seen the image on the tilma as youngsters, some dating back to 1590, also testified that the colors and the image were as vivid in 1666 as they recalled them being in their youth. The experts considered this a miraculous event, especially considering the very humid and saline environment to which the tilma had been exposed for all those years.

The professor's findings were also in relative conformance with statements from other witnesses who viewed and reported on the cloth in prior years. In 1648, for example, Miguel Sánchez had inspected the fabric of the tilma and noted that the material is actually two cloaks woven together by a cotton thread, commonly referred to as an ayatl. This construction, he added, is consistent with the tradition that it was made from a poor Indian's cloak. This finding presented an initial problem, however, as Juan Diego was not considered to be poor for his time. That dilemma was resolved when, a year later in 1649, Luis Lasso de la Vega viewed the tilma, reporting "that in the sixteenth century only wealthy Indians dressed in cotton garments."[123] Lasso de la Vega also measured the dimensions of the cloth, noting that its height from head to toe is fifty-two inches.

Chapter 13
Eighteenth Century Investigations of the Tilma

1751 to 1756

About eighty-five years later, on April 30, 1751, seven of the finest painters in Mexico were on a quest to determine if it were possible for any man to have the technical ability to paint the image of Our Lady of Guadalupe on the tilma of Juan Diego. Among those who gathered in the sanctuary of Guadalupe to examine the image with its protective glass removed were Miguel Cabrera, José de Ibarra, Patricio Morlete Ruiz, Manuel Osorio, and Francisco Antonio Vallejo. They never doubted that the image was a painting. In fact, they presupposed it to be one that used oil and tempera paints. Their conclusions were consistent with others before them who said that it was not possible for the image to have been painted on this coarse cloth by any man. The conclusions of this investigation were published in 1756 by the most celebrated of Mexican painters, Miguel Cabrera. The report, a total of eight paragraphs that were each the length of chapters, was published "after [he] presented it to the other artists for their approval, with the title *Maravilla Americana.*"[124] The key points of the report follow:

1. The cloth of the tilma should have been decayed years earlier by the humidity and saline winds driven off the lake. Further, the fragility of the single cotton thread holding together the two heavy pieces of the tilma should have never lasted for over two hundred years.

2. The cloth's composition has a "coarse weave of threads commonly called pita, which the Indians took from palms native to this country, from which they made their poor cloaks, which they called ayatl, and we now commonly call ayate."[125] Cabrera also notes an anomaly in the composition of the cloth. Though the cloth is made of ordinary material rough in texture, it is "smooth to the touch like fine silk, such as he has felt on many occasions. No other ayates have this quality."[126]

3. The area of the tilma on which the image appears had not been prepared in any way, shape, or form. Specifically, no sizing was applied to the tilma. This is something that would have been essential for paint to adhere on coarse material. Cabrera is clear on this point as the use of sizing would prevent an image from seeping through the material to the other side, yet he notes that the "colors could be seen on the reverse side in all their vividness."[127]

4. The appearance of the image is symmetrical and in good proportion, in accordance with the fundamental principles of art. In Cabrera's judgement, "there is no contour that is not miraculous."[128] He determined the woman in the image to be about fourteen or fifteen years of age based on the proportions of the head, an assessment which supports Becerra Tanco's testimony of almost one hundred years earlier. Yet, the height of the image, at four feet, eight inches, is proportional to the average height of an adult woman.

5. The group's visual analysis indicates that four types of paint were used on the painting, oil (used on the head, hands, tunic, and the angel with clouds); tempera (temple) (used for the mantle); gouache (aguazo) (used for the field beneath the rays surrounding the Virgin) and labrada al temple (used in the rays themselves). These four types are used in combination in the image, a virtual impossibility since conflicting types of preparation are essential for each technique. Cabrera calls the use of all four types in a single painting "unprecedented and miraculous," leading him to believe the work to be of supernatural origin.

6. "Oil paints need sizing in order to bind to cloth, though Cabrera has said the tilma has no such sizing. Tempera, the most ancient form of painting, refers not to a specific paint material but to the technique of mixing (tempering) colors with a binding medium, usually a gum or egg yolk. Gouache (called aguazo in baroque Spanish), like tempera, mixes pigment with binding medium, but results in an impermanent paint that can be dissolved by water. Gouache paint is applied to a moistened canvas. Pintura labrada al temple is a two-stage process. First, a white egg tempera is applied, and then color is overlaid on top. The white of this last technique

is what other observers, before and after Cabrera, have mistaken for sizing."[129]

Mixing these styles would require treating various parts of the cloth differently, risking the complete destruction of other parts of the cloth. "Accordingly," noted Cabrera, "you could not paint all four styles on the cloth even after great effort."[130] In fact, this feat could not be duplicated by the most prominent painters of the time even when painting on better fabrics and using only oil paint, the easiest paint with which to work.

7. Upon the initial inspection of the cloth by the seven painters, Cabrera records that when he "first saw the gold on the image, he thought it looked like actual gold dust. He describes its color as that which butterflies have in their wings. Yet upon touch, he found that the gold was not superimposed, but incorporated with the weave, as if the cloth had been woven with it. He could see distinctly that all the threads are of gold. Wherever there is gold, its presence is recognizable by touch only by a concavity which feels as if the gold were imprinted."[131] He found this technique unprecedented in any other painting and impossible for a human to do.

8. Cabrera addressed six concerns recognizing theoretical mechanical imperfections in the image. First, it had been noted that the image is in non-conformity with art because "it does not stand with respect to the perpendicular line." Cabrera argues that this is reflective of the fact that no 16th-century Mexican painter understood the rubrics of art. This could easily be corrected by an improved mounting of the tilma in its frame. Second, some said that the portion of the left leg below the knee is too short. Cabrera notes "that this is an

instance of foreshortening (escorzo), as required by the rules of perspective. Since the Virgin is stepping forth with her right foot, the left is withdrawn in the background, and thus appears shorter."[132] The third objection focused on the disproportionality of the hands, which Cabrera attributes to a measuring error, noting that when measured from the base of the palm to the fingertips they are proportionally correct. Likewise, the fourth objection concentrated on the non-symmetrical nature of the right shoulder. In response, "Cabrera measured this carefully, taking into account the Lady's height, as well as the fact that Her body is slanted diagonally, and found that the shoulder is in conformity with good proportion."[133] The fifth objection concerned what appeared to be opposing light sources rather than a distinct source. Cabrera observed, however, that the rays of sun which surround the image materialize as many light sources and consequently make it impossible and undesirable to abide by this standard.

9. Finally, critics had noted that outlining the image constituted poor technique. In fact, Cabrera noted, that many of the features of the image were indeed outlined contrary to what was considered good form in realistic representations ever since the Renaissance, as they detract from the enjoyment of the painting. However, such is not the case with the image of Guadalupe. "On the contrary," Cabrera notes, "it adds a little *'yo no se que de gracia,'* (*I do not know what grace*) which no painter has been able to imitate. In fact,[134] the outlines make the miracle more credible, for no human painter would attempt such a work with outlines, for he would expect it to result in a totally disgraceful painting. Yet all the intelligent professors admire the painting as a masterful work of art."[135]

The report included letters of affirmation from each of the other six painters who participated in the study, confirming that they were in agreement with all that Cabrera had written. Throughout the study, Cabrera touched the image only with great reverence and reluctance indicating that he was probably a devotee of the image prior to making his examination. It is widely accepted, however, that such devotion did not impair his "aesthetic judgement of the image's beauty and the perfection of its contours. While no one doubts that the image is technically sound and indeed beautiful, it is another matter to make it the standard of perfection as Cabrera seems to do, regarding all copies as inferior to the degree that they deviate from it."[136]

A Terrible Accident

In 1785, a worker at the chapel in which the sacred image of Our Lady was kept, carefully lowered the glass encasement holding the tilma onto a table. He never tired of looking at the beautiful image of Our Lady up close. He carefully and reverently opened the case, exposing the inside of the glass once again. As he prepared to apply the fifty percent nitric acid solution onto the encasement, his hand slipped, causing a considerable quantity of the solvent to spill onto the tilma and a large portion of the image itself.

Though the nitric acid solution was powerful enough to erase the image and eat away a portion of the cloth instantaneously, there was very little damage. In fact, the minimal damage caused by the spill disappeared almost entirely as the image self-restored over the ensuing thirty days, leaving only minor stains on parts of the tilma not containing the image.

Artists Attempt to Replicate the Image

Virtually since the appearance of Mary's image on the tilma, many prominent artists tried to replicate it. Even when using only oil paint on very high-quality canvas, no one was able to come close to replicating the image without tracing it. It was common practice during this period in artistic history to replicate masterpieces by sight. The masters of the day were so adept at doing this that frequently it was difficult to distinguish between the original and the copy.

Replication of the image of Our Lady of Guadalupe on Juan Diego's tilma was something attempted with relative regularity. In December of 1786, Dr. José Ignacio Bartolache was granted permission to inspect the image and did so alone, examining the tilma without its protective glass covering. He found the cloth to be not rough, but rather fine and well-woven. Dr. Bartolache was a scholar of medicine and physics, not a painter, but his amazement at the craftsmanship employed in painting the image gave him an idea.

Consequently, in January of 1787 he was again allowed to inspect the image. This time he was accompanied by five highly accomplished and accredited painters who assisted him. Two of these men, Andrés López and Rafael Gutierrez, were tasked with painting a replica of the image on similar cloth (iczotl cloth) and using the painting techniques of tempera, oil and aguazo. The pair worked on their respective paintings from February 6 to March 14, 1787, and though the copies were beautiful, they were very different than the original. "Even after making exceptional arrangements to replicate the tilma, Bartolache attests that the two copies were altogether dissimilar from the original, both in drawing and in the mode of painting."[137] Following this exercise, the masters all agreed "that the holy image was miraculously painted."[138]

Many exceptional master painters tried to paint duplicates of the image of Our Lady of Guadalupe, but not could come close to recreating the beauty of the heavenly portrait causing many to comment that the original could not have been painted by human hands. This image was painted by a Peruvian master painter.

Chapter 14
Twentieth Century Investigations of the Tilma

Scientific Discoveries Enhance the Miraculous Nature of the Image 1929-1949

From the inception of the 1531 painting on Juan Diego's tilma, through the early years of the twentieth century, the only studies performed on the cloth were examinations of its composition and analysis of the types of paints used to create it. That would not change for another hundred and forty-two years when in 1929, Alfonso Marcué González, a photographer of the Basilica of Guadalupe, examined the enlarged negatives and photographs that were taken of the image. To his amazement, he discovered what appeared to be the "clear image of a bearded man reflected in the right eye" of the Virgin.

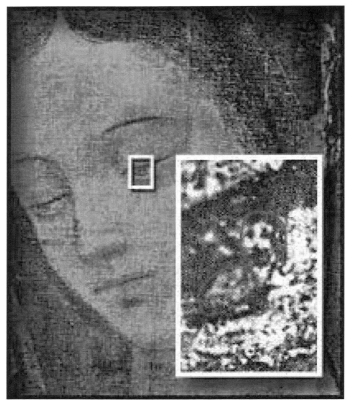

Photographer Alfonso Marcue Gonzales enlarged photographs of the image in 1929 and discovered the reflection of a bearded man in the right eye of the Virgin.

Marcué González had no doubts about what he had seen and decided to bring the information to the authorities at the Basilica. He was told, however, that he should maintain complete silence about the discovery pending further investigation. He complied but made note of it in his private writing. Not much would be heard about the reflection for another twenty-two years as "the matter was eventually shelved and then forgotten."[139]

In 1936, however, it was decided that a histological and chemical analysis were also necessary to further trace the origins of this masterpiece. For a ten-year span of time beginning in 1936, two such analyses were performed, the only two known to exist, and information on them is scarce.

The first of these was performed by the abbot of the Basilica of Guadalupe, don Feliciano Cortés Mora. He gave some threads from the tilma to Saltillo bishop Francisco de Jesús María Echavarría for his reliquary. Bishop Echavarría, in turn, provided two fiber strands, a red and a yellow, to college student Ernesto Sodi Pallares,[140] requesting that Pallares have them tested outside of Mexico.

Pallares contacted his close friend Marcelino García Junco, professor emeritus of organic chemistry at the National University of Mexico (UNAM), for advice on how to proceed with the request. Junco had received his doctorate in Germany and while there, befriended biochemist Richard Kuhn, who, two years later, would be Nobel Laureate. Junco knew what to do. He sent "a letter of introduction and recommendation to Dr. Kuhn on behalf of Fritz Hahn, a German academic residing in Mexico who had been invited by the Nazi party to attend the Olympic Games in Munich. Hahn would bring the fibers to Kuhn for analysis."[141]

Pallares indicated that the lab results sent to him in Mexico suggested that "the chemical composition of the fiber coloring did not match any natural mineral, vegetable, or animal pigment. The results were, however, 'consistent with a variety of synthetic pigments, yet these were all invented in the late nineteenth century or later.'"[142]

The lack of clear and precise documentation on this test make the results questionable. Regardless, the result of this analysis and the studies performed by the painters before it, lead to two tentative conclusions. First, no human painter was capable of painting the image on the tilma, and second, the pigments used to paint the image did not exist in the sixteenth century.

Ten years later, in 1946, UNAM performed chemical and microscopic examinations of the cloth in the hope of reaching a determination as to the composition, not of the pigments of the paint, but of the tilma itself. Previous studies determined the composition to be iczotl, biologically known as *Palma Silvestre* or *Yucca Aloifolia*, but illustrious art scholar Manuel Toussaint considered the cloth "to be much too fine to be woven maguey."[143]

Consequently, Toussaint asked biologist Isaac Ochoterena, the honorary director of the Institute of Biology, to analyze fibers from a piece of the tilma. Ochoterena, a highly accomplished specialist in plant histology, secured a cloth fragment measuring eight mm by five mm from a reliquary in the care of Lic. D. Benigno Ugarte. In the presence of photographer D. Alfonso Marcué González, Guadalupan scholar Lic. D. Manuel Garibi Tortolero, and professor D. Abelardo Carrillo y Gariel, Ugarte opened the reliquary and Ochoterena took three milligrams of fibers from the remnant while González snapped photographs of the fabric.

Upon inspection, Ochoterena noted that the cloth fragment "appeared coarse like a sack, and the removed fibers had a dressing (aderezo), part of which must have been flaxseed (linaza),"[144] a common component of oil paint. Flaxseed, however, is not used in sizing because it causes fabric to decay. This is further evidence that sizing was not used on the cloth prior to painting, adding to the remarkable nature of the image.

He also performed a few histochemical tests followed by a chemical analysis of the fibers. The results of these tests showed that "the cloth is made of a species of agave [of an indeterminate species],* commonly known as maguey.

---

* *A report issued by Drs. Ernesto Sodi Pallares and Roberto Palacios Bermudez in 1976 indicates that "the species of agave used in the tilma was A. Popotule, a variation of A. Lechuguilla. They note that past investigators may have confused this plant with the yucca palm called izote (iczotle). Its strong, flexible fibers were used to make hats and blankets for the poor. The finished woven product is rough, hard and resistant. Notably, the side that receives more light becomes smooth and soft over time. This is consistent with what has been observed of the tilma's texture on its painted side." – From* http://www.arcaneknowledge.org/catholic/guadalupe12.htm, *Part XIII, page 14.*

The Ochoterena study of 1946 remains to this day the most re-liable histochemical analysis performed on a fragment of the tilma. All other technical analysis used to determine "the composition of the cloth, are based on ocular or low-power microscopic examination, without any chemical analysis or precise measurement."[145]

The year 1946 also ushered in a new wave of reviews on the tilma, this time focusing on photographic inspections. They began as early as March when authorized photographer Jesús Cataño Wilhelmy took thirty-four plates of the image over a period of two nights, using a type of black-and-white film, called panchromatic film, that is sensitive to all wavelengths of visible light. The photographs of the image were taken both with and without the protective glass covering. Many of the photographs were taken through color filters, as Cataño Wilhelmy hoped to reproduce the exact colors of the image on the tilma.

This technique enabled the photographer to distinguish with clarity which areas of the image had been retouched over the years, as the restorers could not have created an identical match of the orig-inal colors.*[146] Curiously, Cataño Wilhelmy discovered that the face had a yellow brilliance that appeared in photographs, but was not perceptible "to the naked eye, meaning that the painter used bright rather than dark colors to show relief or texture, which is contrary to established technique for shading."[147]

The experiment indicated to Wilhelmy that "most of the face was still original, except for retouches on the forehead, nose, cheekbone, and tip of the chin. These were perhaps justified by the darkening caused by candle smoke in the upper part of the image. Similarly, he saw that the cloak, though mostly original, had been retouched in the area of the head. Through a blue filter, he could discern a horizontal line, curved downward, of a change in tone, probably corresponding to where the crown had once been. He also saw a reddish spike extending from the apparent crown, matching a color found in some of the surrounding rays, which were now mostly overlaid with gold." - From http://www.arcane-knowledge.org/catholic/guadalupe12.htm, Part XIII, page 15. (For more infor-mation see endnotes.)

Cataño Wilhelmy could not provide a scientific explanation for this, since the "human eye would not be able to distinguish shades of yellow sufficiently well to make a textured image thereby."[148] In a later interview, Cataño Wilhelmy also noted that the "color of the Virgin's face changed with the distance of the observer, even under constant illumination." Even a short, two-foot alteration in distance produced this effect. The occurrence was also observed independently by his co-worker, lithographer Alfonso Martínez de Velasco, who noted that the face had a reddish appearance when viewed from up close. Even Cataño Wilhelmy's brother, Eduardo Cataño Wilhemy, a painter by profession, confirmed the phenomenon. What they found equally astounding is that white light turned the colors a shade of gray rather than causing them to brighten. Cataño Wilhelmy tried to produce these effects using other paintings but was unable to duplicate them.

Don Joaquin Flores used high quality photographs in his painstaking 1946 study of the image and reported his findings in December. He could detect the stain on the right side of the tilma where nitric acid had been spilled in the late 1700s. He could also detect a reddish coloration in the lower left which he attributed to be remnants "of some painted roses that are said to have been added to the lower portion as an embellishment, much like the cherubim that were later erased."[149] He also pointed out a variety of small round stains. These he attributed to candle wax.

Flores also noted the following:

1. There are countless stains on the field of 122 rays which is made of dirty yellow ochre. The discolorations, which are more pronounced around the head, are attributable to the patina or unintentional abuse. Some of the rays are straight while others are wavy, and they are separated by different distances with the rays on the right side being closer

together. The thickness of each ray also differs from one to the other.

2. The face of the image is slightly browner than pearl with very little contrast, easily resulting in alterations to the face's aspect, particularly in the area of the cheek and forehead.

3. The hands have small horizontal stains including stains on the fingers of the left hand.

4. The belt seems to have darkened from the original purple to a brown-black color.

5. The original salmon color of the tunic remains, but there are many small round stains on the darker part of it, particularly to the area below the knee. The most significant discoloration of the tunic is at the bottom. The tunic is also outlined with two black lines, each the thickness of a hair. He agrees with other experts who contend that no human could have made such delicate lines on a surface as coarse as the tilma without first applying a sizing to it. This, of course, was not done.

6. The nose and eyebrows of the angel are those of an adult, yet the angel remains childlike in all other aspects. Its wings are white, blue and reddish in appearance and the entire angel is very well preserved. He notes that earlier observers have re-marked the image of the angel is also supernatural in nature.

7. Regardless of the various stains and imperfections seen though extreme closeup, the image when viewed from a distance remains beautiful in every way. Any deterioration is attributable to the fact that for the first one hundred and forty

years, the image was unprotected rather than being encased in glass, allowing thousands of people to touch and kiss it, and to light candles near it. The salty and humid air is also blamed for the discoloration. Yet, Flores believes the overall state of preservation to be miraculous.

A year later, in 1947, New York journalist Coley Taylor observed the image from both near and far. His assessment concurred with that of Flores, noting that "many details of the image were more easily seen from a distance than up close, contrary to logical expectation. The stars are radiant from a distance," he said, "though barely discernible up close. Even the colors change, as the sea-green cloak becomes dark blue when viewed up close. The tunic is a faint pink up close but becomes shadowed from a distance. The face appears light up close but becomes shadowed from a distance."[150] And the differences did not affect only the color. Taylor went on to describe how, in defiance of all logic, the figure seems larger when viewed at a distance. No other masterpiece viewed by Taylor in museums and private collections produced these same effects.

In this same year, Manuel Garibi Tortolero, a researcher who studied the image of Our Lady of Guadalupe extensively, noted that the photographic plates taken by Jesús Cataño Wilhelmy a year earlier prove that no sizing or primer was used under the paint. He further stressed that multiple techniques were not used in creating the image, contradicting the earlier assertions of the baroque painters, but contends, rather, that the original image is tempera while oil was used later only in the areas that were touched up. He goes on to make the incredible claim that the tempera paint was applied "in a single step. It was not properly painted but imprinted or stamped on the tilma by the flowers, for which reason it has natural pigments."[151] For proof he points to the fact that there are no brush strokes on the image. Further, he notes that the colors are incorporated "in individual threads, sometimes forming figures thereby, as in a tap-estry, while in other places the pigment dust seems to have been pressed into the cloth."[152]

In 1949, Abbot Feliciano Cortés Mora, who had on many occasions viewed and touched the tilma, affirmed in the basilica's official newsletter that the cloth is smooth to the touch. He con-firmed the dimensions of the portion of the cloth exposed by the 168-x-105-centimeter frame. Most notably, Mora "acknowledges that the image has suffered some retouches, and these retouches have deteriorated over time. Examples of this are at the union of the two cloths and in the gold rays which someone had foolishly tried to brighten." He notes how someone, most likely a pious relic-seeker, cut a small hole in the neck of the tunic near its close.

1951 – 1979

Historian Helen Behrens viewed the tilma without the glass in 1951. Sixty-one witnesses, including a young painter, attended the examination. Her statement confirms the testimony given by those before her who acknowledged that the colors seem more vivid when viewed from a distance. She noted that the gold veins in the tunic were more pronounced because of the black border that sur-rounds them. She made particular note of the rosy cheeks of the Vir-gin's face and the black hair that protrudes from under Her veil. The beauty of the Lady's face, she said, cannot be duplicated in art and can be almost captured only in the best photographs. Like others before her, she had a difficult time classifying the types of paint used, "as it simultaneously exhibits traits of oil, tempera, watercolor and pastel."[153]

On May 29 of that same year, a draughtsman by the name of José Carlos Salinas Chávez conducted his own examination of the photographs of the tilma. As he examined a large photograph of Our Lady's face with a powerful magnifying glass, his hand moved across the right eye. Salinas Chávez stopped. He saw something but couldn't believe what it was. He allowed a moment for his own eyes to focus and then took a second, closer look. He observed what appeared to him to be the reflection of a man's head. In fact, it was an obscure image of a bust of a man with a beard.

Salinas Chávez published his findings, unleashing a flurry of speculation. Mexico City Archbishop Luis Marie Martínez established a special commission to investigate the image further. That commission was expanded by Archbishop Miguel Darío Miranda, involving the participation of more than twenty physicians and ophthalmologists, inviting them to examine the image.

While at a routine medical appointment with his eye doctor, Javier Torroella Bueno, Salinas Chávez happened to mention what he discovered in the eye of the Virgin. "It's physically impossible," the ophthalmologist told him, "for an image to have been reflected in Mary's eyes."[154] However, he agreed to check the photographs for himself to prove that his patient had been mistaken. Dr. Torroella Bueno, an esteemed ophthalmologist of the day, studied the several photographs of the image on the tilma provided by Salinas Chávez and was stunned to discover that there were indeed images hidden within the eyes of the Virgin. In a report, Torroella Bueno observed "what seems to be the presence of the triple reflection (Samson-Purkinje effect) characteristic of all live human eyes and states that the resulting images are located exactly where they are supposed to be according to such effect, and also that the distortion of the images agree with the curvature of the cornea."[155]

Dr. Torroella Bueno added:

"If we take a square piece of paper and place it in front of the eye, we realize that the cornea is not flat (nor is it spherical) for a distortion of the image is produced which is a function of the place of the cornea, where it is reflected. [Furthermore, if the paper is moved to a certain distance, it is also reflected] in the counter lateral corner of the other eye, that is to say, if an image is reflected in the temporal region of the right eye, it will be reflected in the nasal region of the left eye. The experiment is verified in our image, in inverse conditions: the silhouette of the same bearded man is reflected in the nasal region of the right eye and also appears in the temporal corner of the left eye. The distortion of the reflected image is even more striking, for it is in perfect obedience to the laws of curvature of the cornea."[156]

What surprised Dr. Torroella Bueno even more than these observations is the fact that Mary's eyes, "reacted like the eyes of a live person."[157] He published the results of his study in 1958.

When the Commission finally concluded its work, it published its findings, confirming the discovery of Salinas Chávez, "together with the dramatic disclosure that the human face in the eye of Our Lady had been positively identified from a contemporary painting as that of Juan Diego."[158]

While the Commission labored for five years, others had been satisfying their own curiosity regarding the things that they had been reading about the tilma. In 1952, Nicolas Mariscal, an architect by profession, examined the cloth, paying particular attention to the fusion of light and shade. He noted that the fusion was seamless and portrayed a "masterful moderation and subtlety in their use. This yielded the effect of volume, not of an opaque illuminated body, but of a refulgent one."[159] Mariscal spoke of the clear tonal contrasts used in painting the image. These are often used to suggest the volume and modelling of the subjects depicted. Known as chiaroscuro in the world of art, this technique was mastered by such renowned artists as Leonardo da Vinci and Caravaggio. Mariscal also verified that there was neither varnish nor sizing used in the painting, except in the areas that were retouched, making the previously noted effects of chiaroscuro even more remarkable an occurrence.

In the years that passed since 1951 when Helen Behrens had first inspected the image, her curiosity grew more insatiable. Unable to provide satisfactory answers for the image's origin, she contacted internationally known master painter Francisco Camps Ribera. At her behest, he conducted a study of the image on the tilma in 1954. This Barcelona professor was granted permission to observe the tilma on April 14 but was forced to view it from inside its glass case. Viewing the image with a strong magnifying glass, Camps Ribera could find no brushstrokes. Neither could he find any evidence that the cloth had been properly prepared for painting.

All paintings will betray the artists brush strokes when viewed up close or under magnification, even the DaVinci's Mona Lisa hanging in the Louvre. The image of Our Lady of Guadalupe on the tilma, however, has no evidence of brush strokes even when viewed under powerful magnification and modern ophthalmologic equipment.

Over the years, Camps Ribera had examined thousands of paintings in private collections and in museums alike. He had travelled throughout Europe and North America to do so and in all his practice, nothing more than a mere visual inspection had been needed for him to identify the technique used in a painting whether it was oil, watercolor, tempera, or something else. That was not the case with this inspection, however. His many years of experience and all his expertise proved useless in determining how this image was made. At the conclusion of his review, he determined it would have been impossible for any human to have painted the image on the cloth under these conditions. He knew that "no Spanish, Flemish or Italian painter residing in Mexico demonstrated sufficient sensibility or technique."[160] He also noted that it would have been "incredible for any of three Indian painters who worked for the Franciscans – Marcos Cipac, Pedro Chachalaca or Francisco Xinamamal – [to have] represented the Virgin in such an authentic Christian spirit, as they were all recent converts from a very different religion."[161]

Camps Ribera pointed out several other oddities, including:

1. Every other four-hundred-year-old painting is cracked with age, has lifted paint, and/or is darkened with a tobacco color. The image on the tilma shows no aging and still bears vivid colors that have very distinctive contrasts unless viewed up close with a magnifying glass, in which case the colors appear dull. These attributes are unique to this image of Our Lady of Guadalupe.

2. His measurements do not comport to the dimensions of the cloth noted by others. Camps Ribera measured the cloth to be 104 cm in width, a number right between the 103 cm measurement taken in 1951 by Helen Behrens and the 105 cm measurement noted by Garibi Tortolero in 1947. He also

pointed out that while the Virgin measures 56 inches tall, she appears larger when the image is viewed at a distance.

Shortly after Torroella Bueno's revelation, Dr. Rafael Torija Lavoignet, another noted ophthalmologist, was able to examine the eyes of the image using an ophthalmoscope, an instrument that allows a doctor to see inside the fundus of the eye. He performed three detailed examinations on February 16, February 20, and May 26, 1958. The doctor "observed the apparent human figure in the corneas of both eyes, with the location and distortion of a normal human eye and specially noted a unique appearance of the eyes: they look strangely 'alive' when examined,"[162] he said. They were nothing like the eyes of the Madonna on paintings by Raphael, Murillo, or Van Dyck.

Dr. Lavoignet explained what he observed to Brother Bruno Bonnet-Eymard this way:

> "I examined the image with a powerful magnifying glass... I did not know that a human bust had been discovered in the eyes of the Guadalupa. I observed with the greatest attention and indeed, I noticed that a human bust is to be seen in the cornea of both eyes. I looked first in the right eye and then in the left. Surprised, I thought it was necessary to examine the fact by means of scientific procedures." (Dr. Lavoignet then undertook a meticulous examination of the eyes with an ophthalmoscope.) "In the cornea of the eyes, a human bust can be seen. The distortion and place of the optical image are identical with what is produced in a normal eye. When the light of the ophthalmoscope is directed onto the pupil of a human eye, a light reflection is seen to shine on its outer circle. By following this reflection and by suitably changing the

lenses of the ophthalmoscope, it is possible to obtain the image at the back of the eye. By directing the ophthalmoscope light onto the pupil of the eye of the image of the Virgin, the same light reflection appears. As a consequence of this reflection, the pupil lights up in a diffused manner, giving the impression of hollow relief...This reflection is impossible to obtain on a flat surface and one, moreover, that is opaque as is this picture. I then examined by means of the ophthalmoscope the eyes of various paintings, both in oils and watercolor and those of photographs. On none of them, all of different people, was the least reflection to be seen, whereas the eyes of the Blessed Virgin of Guadalupe give the impression of life."[163]

The fascinating account of Dr. Lavoignet's exciting discovery continues in the words of Brother Bruno: "It all looks as though a light ray were entering a cavity, filling out a volumetric ocular globe, radiating from within a diffuse light. I did the experiment myself with an ophthalmoscope. The bronze, hazel-colored eye of the Blessed Virgin lights up, and on the surface there shines quite distinctly the silhouette of a human bust. The head is turned three-quarters towards the Virgin's right and slightly bent forward; the chest is framed and lengthened by a movement of the arms going forward as though to show something. It all happened as though, at the moment of the image being impressed, a man who was facing the Blessed Virgin, and reflected in the cornea of her eye, had himself been *photographed* in this indirect way. There is more. The image of this bust shows a distortion in exact conformity with the laws of such a reflection *in vivo*."[164]

The news of these reports swept Mexico by storm and the impact was stunning. It was as if the tilma of Juan Diego acted as "exposed color film which had photographed the Virgin (albeit invisible to the human eye) at the very moment when he was reflected in her eyes – an incredible fact which has lain concealed for over four hundred years and has at last been revealed and confirmed by modern science!"[165]

The discoveries of Dr. Bueno and Dr. Lavoignet were confirmed over the ensuing years by many ophthalmologists including Ismael Ugalde Nieto, Jaime Palacios, Guillermo Silva Rivera, and Ernestina Zavaleta.

As earthshattering as this new information was, the amazing discoveries hidden in the tilma, and revealed only through the invention of modern medical equipment and scientific processes, were to continue. In 1962, an American doctor, Charles Wahlig, O.D., and his wife Isabelle, conducted their own study in which they enlarged a photograph twenty-five times. They noticed two additional images reflected in the eyes of the Virgin and published the result in a report dated September 1963, also referencing the Sanson-Purkinje effect. They successfully reconstructed the precise conditions under which the "celestial portrait" came about. Charles Wahlig explained:

> "Our son-in-law, Edward Gebhardt, has a great deal of experience with photography techniques and suggested two possible ways of making the reproduction. The first was to photograph the eye at short range and obtain clearly visible reflections of people situated in front of the eye. The second method was to photograph a person at a distance of several feet, next enlarge the photograph until the eye filled the picture, then study the reflections of the people confronting the person whose eye was being

photographed. We decided that the first pictures should be taken using the first method. With a camera especially constructed for taking close-up photographs, we took pictures of our family arranged similarly to the way we believe the original scene existed as portrayed in Our Lady's eye which is photographed in the pictures. My wife, myself and our daughter Mary took the positions in front of Mary, and our reflections appear in the cornea of her eye.

At the time when Juan Diego presented the bishop with the flowers, Our Lady was actually present in the room, but chose to remain invisible. Instead, in order to give a visible, lasting indication of her presence, she chose to imprint upon Juan Diego's blanket an authentic picture of herself as she stood there watching the scene. The picture is complete in every detail, even to the reflections in her eye of Juan Diego and two other people standing near him and someone apparently looking over his shoulder. It seems from the posture of Juan Diego and the other two that they were not aware of Our Lady's presence. The two appear to be looking at Juan Diego and he, we may assume, is looking at the bishop."[166]

Perhaps the most amazing detail about the reflections in the eyes of the Blessed Mother is that scientific verification was not even possible until the invention of the camera in the 1800s, over 250 years after the image appeared on the tilma of Juan Diego. It was impossible, therefore, for anyone living in 1531 to have fabricated such an illusion.

The following year, in 1963, Camps Ribera performed another examination of the cloth, his second in nine years. This time he deduced that the black outlines had been added at a later date and, by looking at the few remaining lines of the crown, was able to determine that the crown feature was not original to the image. He also remarked, after comparing the color of the moon to that of the bow beneath the Virgin's hands, that the dark brown color of the moon on the tilma has not been altered, even though it would have been more typical of the period to paint it gold or silver.

In 1974 and 1975, Mexican ophthalmologist Enrique Graue confirmed the earlier findings. After looking at the inner part of the eyes of the Virgin through an endoscope he stated that he "could not get rid of the impression that it was a supernatural phenomenon. When using the ophthalmoscope, he at times wanted to ask Mary to look upwards a little, because Her eyes were so like those of a live person."[167]

In August 1975, Mexican surgeon Amado Jorge Kuri examined the eyes of the Virgin and "published a formal expert opinion. He too noticed the Sanson-Purkinje effect, and he acknowledged that one could discern in the irises a male figure with a clearly visible head, neck, and right hand. Summing up, he declared that Mary's eyes, though it seemed to be absurd, did indeed look like those of a live person."[168]

Later that year, in December, Dr. Eduardo Turati Alvarez conducted his own examination of the photographs. An ophthalmologist by profession, Dr. Turati Alvarez used the best photographic equipment possible, made available to him by the Kodak company. The Doctor concluded "that the image in the Madonna's eyes gave one the impression that it was 'stuck' or 'printed' on the fabric, and not painted."[169] He was also able to detect two, somewhat smaller figures standing beside the bearded man in Mary's eyes.

Many additional studies of the eyes of the Virgin have taken place since the startling discovery of Dr. Rafael Torija Lavoignet in 1956. The basic conclusions of all agree. There are two, however, that are of particular note.

On May 7, 1979 a professor at the University of Florida attempted to answer the burning question surrounding the mystery of the image on the tilma – is it "possible to demonstrate physically the supernatural origin of the sacred image?"[170]

Philip Serna Callahan conducted an infrared analysis, perhaps the most important examination performed for use in tracing the historic roots of the image. Inspired by recent examinations of the Shroud of Turin, widely thought to be the burial cloth of Jesus of Nazareth, Florida professor Jody Brant Smith and Monsignor Enrique Salazar of the Basilica invited Dr. Callahan to the Basilica to perform the examination and infrared analysis. Dr. Callahan was not only a biophysicist, but was also an experienced painter and an expert in infrared photography. Though Callahan's work was financed by a private company founded by Professor Jody Brant Smith who, in her words, hoped "to bring together religion and science"[171] for this study, the work and the findings are Callahan's alone.

In order to conduct his experiment, Callahan was granted authorization to photograph the image outside of its glass and metal reliquary. He could not touch the cloth and was allowed access only from nine o'clock in the evening until midnight. He took something on the order of sixty photographs of the image, many in infrared radiation, hoping to discern "if there was a preliminary artist's drawing under the picture. Other photographs were computer-enhanced and studied for clues as to the image's origin."[172]

Infrared photography is considered the most wide-ranging technique used in the study of old paintings and written records to determine their historical origin, method of composition and authenticity. It can detect over-paintings and alterations because all pigments vary in the way they reflect and transmit infrared light. Dr. Callahan noted in his report that "no study of a work of art can be considered complete until the techniques of infrared photography have been utilized. And certainly, no valid scientific study is complete without such an analysis."[173]

The infrared examination uncovered a startling and disturbing fact. There was no trace of paint in the fabric. Nor had it been treated with any kind of sizing technique. Callahan was without words to explain how this could happen. How is it "possible that, despite the fact there is no paint, the colors maintain their luminosity and brilliance?"[174] he wondered.

According to José Aste Tönsmann, a Peruvian engineer familiar with the study, Callahan "showed how the image changes in color slightly according to the angle of viewing, a phenomenon that is known by the word iridescence, a technique that cannot be reproduced with human hands."[175] For example, Callahan found that the Virgin's face exhibits life-like qualities, especially in and around the mouth, "where a coarse fiber elevated above the lip, [imparts] a three-dimensional aspect. Similar effects occur below the left cheek and to the right of and below the right eye."[176] Callahan acknowledged that these things could not be done by any person or artist regardless of his level of talent. "It is impossible that any human painter could have selected a tilma with the imperfections of its weave so precisely positioned as to accentuate the shadows and highlights, in order to convey such realism,"[177] he wrote.

The light diffraction is another area that intrigues Callahan and Smith. The report noted that when "viewed up close, the face and hands are a grey-white color which gradually becomes olive as one backs away – an impossible accomplishment for any human painter."[178] He further observed that the colors of the image remain "brilliant and fresh" and that some colors, such as those in the pink robe, defy logic because they are transparent to infrared light while most pink pigments are opaque to such light.

Dr. Callahan concluded that "studying the image was the most moving experience of my life. Just getting that close, I got the same strange feeling that others did who worked on the Shroud of Turin. I believe in logical explanations up to a point. But there is no logical explanation for life. You can break life down into atoms, but what comes after that? Even Einstein said God."[179]

Dr. Aste Tönsmann picked up a copy of the magazine *Vision* and flipped to a story that intrigued him. The article told of several studies in which human figures were detected within the eyes of the image of Our Lady of Guadalupe on a 16th-century tilma worn by Mexican Indian native Juan Diego. Tönsmann felt a shiver of excitement. If such a detailed discovery had been made with but a magnifying glass, then much greater possibilities awaited anyone who had access to the most up-to-date computer technology. Tönsmann decided to undertake his own study, which he did in 1979, using sophisticated image processing techniques with digitized photographs of both eyes. Upon completion of the digitized study, he disclosed that he detected at least four human figures reflected in the eyes of the Virgin. Dr. Tönsmann continued to study the image for the next twenty years.

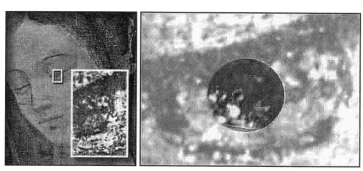

Fascinated by the work of others, Dr. Aste Tonsmann used sophisticated image processing techniques which revealed the presence of four people reflected in the eye of the Virgin.

1980 – 1999

The inexplicable circumstances hidden within the tilma did not conclude with the studies undertaken and completed through 1979, however. In 1981, Fr. Mario Rojas Sánchez had a notion to study how the stars were arranged on the Mantle of Mary's image on the tilma. He solicited the help of Dr. Juan Romero Hernán de Illescas, an astronomer who had his own observatory. Their research took the entire year and employed the use of "specialist computer programming [that] enabled reconstruction of star systems that were visible at any given moment in the past, and from any given point on earth."[180] The study demonstrated that the arrangement of the stars on the tilma were an exact match to the alignment of the stars that appeared over the Mexico City sky on the evening of December 12, 1531 at 6:45 the following morning. According to the Nican Mopohua, the oldest document known to exist on the apparitions of Our Lady of Guadalupe, that was the exact time when Juan Diego exposed his tilma to Bishop Zumárraga. Had he unfurled the tilma as little as five minutes earlier or later, the sky above would have been different. For example, it was only at 6:45 AM on December 12, 1531, that the Northern Crown constellation (Corona Borealis) was able to adorn the head of the Virgin as it does in the image. As it were, "one can see constellations such as the Great Bear, Canes Venatici (Hunting Dogs), Sorpio, and Coma Berenices (Bernice's Hair). [The most remarkable finding, though, is not the fact that the stars on the mantle conform to the Mexico City sky at the precise time that Juan Diego was exposing the image to the bishop,] it is, rather, that the arrangement is not geocentric, i.e., as if the observer were on the earth, but heliocentric, as if the observer were on the sun, thus the observation point is in the middle of the quincunx – the flower with four petals."[181]

The fact that the Corona Borealis corresponded to Mary's head was of great significance to the priests of the ancient Aztec population, just as it was that the constellation Virgo correspond with Her heart and the constellation Gemini to Her knees. It is also quite telling that the apparition occurred on the winter solstice (December 12 on the Aztec calendar) which to us signifies that each day will be successively longer, but to the Aztecs, was symbolic of "an awakening from death to new life."[182]

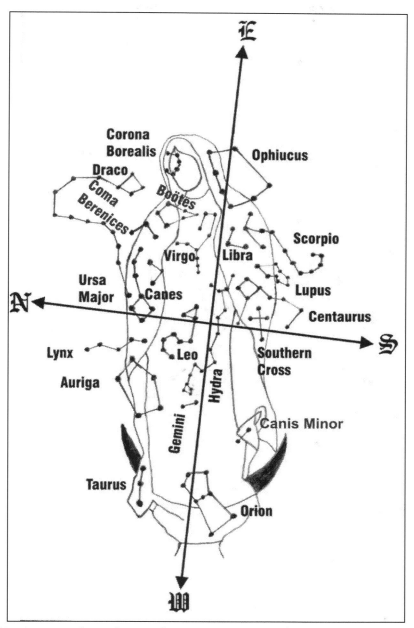

This pictogram shows the star alignment as it appeared over the sky in Mexico City at precisely 6:45 AM on the morning of December 12, 1531.

This amazing discovery was confirmed by two additional Mexican astronomers, Eddie Salazar Gamboa from the Autonomous University of Yucatán and Daniel Flores Gutierrez from the National Autonomous University of Mexico, who used a Redshift 7 computer program to compare the locations of twelve constellations in the image on the tilma with the map of the Mexican sky at exactly 6:45 on the morning of December 12, 1531. Seven of those constellations were completely aligned while two show ninety-five percent, one ninety-nine percent and the last ninety-one percent correspondence.

Dr. Illescas, meanwhile, focused his attention on the mathematical connotations contained in the image, finding that "Our Lady's head is inclined about 23.5 degrees to the right, the same inclination as the earth's equatorial plane to the ecliptic plane."[183] He wondered if this were an accident or an indication or an intentional act of humble "subordination to God in that it was an imitation of the earth's inclination and dependence with regard to the sun."[184] Professor Fernando Ojeda Llanes, a Mexican mathematician from the Yucatán Peninsula, was inspired to apply the writings of the Greek philosopher and mathematician Pythagoras in his analysis of the image. Pythagorean thought was both metaphysical and scientific, including developments in arithmetic, astronomy, geometry, and music. Ojeda Llanes could identify the first three of those elements in the image but could detect no reference to music. To Ojeda Llanes this was troubling, especially since Juan Diego took great pains to mention the music that drew him to Tepeyac Hill where the apparition occurred.

Using a computer monitor, Ojeda Llanes divided the image into two, following the seam of the tilma that split the image. Referencing the forty-six stars that were contained on the image, "he came up with a mathematical model according to which he aligned twenty-three vertical lines on each part of the image. He then transformed the parts into a staff and changed all the stars and flowers

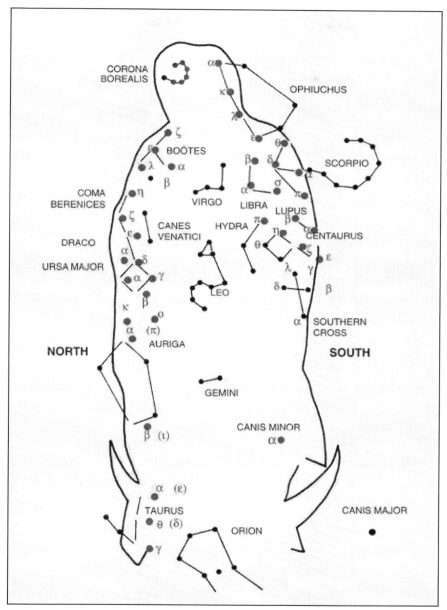

Another pictogram of the star alignment superimposed over the image of Our Lady of Guadalupe.

into notes." The arrangement produced a perfect musical harmony despite being established using a wholly mathematical process. In his disbelief, Ojeda Llanes tried to obtain the same result using the alignment of stars at 6:40 and 6:50 AM on December 12, 1531 rather than at 6:45 AM. "It turned out that even a five-minute difference, and a slight shift of the star constellations, resulted in the computer recording a discordant sound instead of melodic music. Thus, perfect musical harmony could only be achieved when the notes conformed to the arrangement of stars in the original image, and so, in accord with a map of the sky over the capital of Mexico on December 12, 1531 – but only at 6:45 AM."[185] The beautiful musical arrangement produced as a result of Ojeda Llanes experiment can be heard using this link: https://gloria.tv/?embed=frame&height =432&video= 4sRr4YD2QfhpBaLj6zKKfoo7s&width=576.

In 1988, Fr. Rojas Sánchez became intrigued with the layout of the flowers on the Virgin's tunic and decided to undertake an astounding experiment to determine if the layout matched any configurations found in nature. He arranged a map of Mexico on the image with the "quincunx - the flower of the sun – a symbol of divinity and transcendence – on Mary's womb matched to Tepeyac Hill (on the map,) where the apparitions of Our Lady occurred in December 1531. To his amazement, he discovered that some of the mountain flowers on the tunic were in line with certain volcanoes in Mexico." For example, the flowers found on the left sleeve of the tunic correspond directly to the Popocatépetl volcano (17,887 feet) while the one on Her right sleeve corresponds to the Iztaccíhuatl volcano (17,158 feet). Likewise, the flower under Her neck corresponds to the La Malinche volcano (14,635 feet). Further, the star on the right arm of Mary corresponds to the summit of Cerro de Chignautla (8,398 feet) and the one on Her head, to Pico de Orizaba Mountain (18,490 feet). Finally, "the gold-encircled-cross brooch under the neck of the Madonna's tunic corresponds to the summit of Nauhcampatépetl (Place of Four Mountains, 14, 048 feet)."[186]

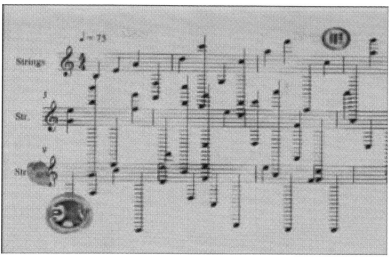

Professore Fernando Ojeda Llanes aligned the stars of the tilma on a musical staff. The result is a beautifully harmonious melody.

Chapter 15
Twenty-First Century Investigations of the Tilma

2000 – 2010

Fr. Sánchez, while amazed, did not quite understand the significance of this "coincidence." Two decades later, however, Professor Fernando Ojeda Llanes reviewed Fr. Rojas Sánchez's work. He found that the degree of alignment between the distinguishing points on the map to the flowers and stars of the tilma was only seventy percent. Rather than dismiss the work, however, Llanes decided to modify the procedures that led to Fr. Rojas Sánchez's conclusions.

Unlike Rojas Sánchez, Ojeda Llanes had access to more accurate satellite mapping programs such as Google Earth. He also aligned the map of Mexico a bit "differently, so that the quincunx corresponded to Cerro de Estrella (Star Mountain), one of the most important geographical points in the Aztec religion, rather than the Virgin's womb. [Llanes reasoned] that it was precisely on this summit that the solar deity cult priests observed whether the sun would rise for the next cycle. When it rose, they lit fires as a sign that the world would continue to exist."[187]

The new study determined that the incidence of alignment of the flowers on the tunic corresponded to the mountain and volcano summits an amazing 92.9 percent. It would have been virtually impossible for sixteenth-century cartographers to have the means to make such a precise map. When this result is applied to the Aztec traditions as part of a pictogram message, and interpreted with the Aztec mentality, the message becomes clear. The Virgin Mother of God "has become part of the Mexican landscape, an intrinsic part of the land. A new Sun has been born of her womb, hence a new era in world history."[188]

Dr. Aste Tonsmann, a researcher from Peru, did not concern himself with things astrological. Rather, he conducted a twenty-year study of the eyes on the miraculous image of the Virgin of Guadalupe with digitized photography. Granted access to the Image without the protective glass, Tonsmann first studied the eyes with a magnifying glass and then took high-quality photographs which he enlarged further. His extensive examination concluded with the release of a report at a conference at the Pontifical Athenaeum Regina Apostolorum in Rome on January 7, 2001. "'Though the dimensions [of the rough maguey fiber fabric of Juan Diego's tilma] are microscopic, the iris and the pupils of the image's eyes have imprinted on them a highly detailed picture of at least thirteen people,' Tonsmann said. 'The same people are present in both the left and right eyes, in different proportions, as would happen when human eyes reflect the objects before them.'"[189]

Tonsmann, who in his research used a digital process similar to that utilized by space probes and satellites when transmitting visual information, noted that the reflection is most likely the still image of the scene on December 12, 1531 at the exact moment that Juan Diego revealed the contents of his tilma to Bishop Zumárraga and the others who were present when the image was revealed. He affirmed his concurrence with those who insist that the image could not have been painted by human hands and cited work of Richard Kuhn, a Nobel Prize winner in chemistry, who found that the image contained no natural, animal or mineral colorings.

In performing his study, Tonsmann "magnified the iris of the Virgin's eyes twenty-five hundred times and, through mathematical and optical procedures, was able to identify all the people imprinted in the eyes."[190] Tonsmann's interpretation of the image is:

"a kneeling Indian with a high forehead, highlighted thanks to his hair being tied back. Indians wore their hair thus in the sixteenth century, as one can see, for instance, in the paintings in the Cerrito Chapel on Tepeyac Hill. His earring is also visible, a local custom of that time.

To the right of the Indian is a bearded man who – according to Tonsmann – is most probably Bishop Juan Zumárraga, as he is very similar to Miguel Cabrera's eighteenth-century painting of him.

Behind the bishop can be seen another man's head, which looks like the bishop's assistant. We know from historical sources that the bishop had a translator, a certain Juan González. In Tonsmann's opinion, it is González who is standing behind the bishop.

Juan Diego – according to Tonsmann – is sideways, wearing a conical hat. Drawings in the sixteenth-century *Codex Mendoza* depict Indians wearing the same sort of hat.

The fifth person is a black woman. Her presence in New Spain in 1531 would seem to have been highly improbable to some, but we know from documents that Hernán Cortés took African slaves with him to America. It also seems not to be insignificant that Bishop Juan Zumárraga left instructions in his will to free two servants, black slaves, after his death – husband and wife, Mary and Pedro.

The sixth figure, on the right, is a bearded man. His figure, on account of being closest to the observer, seems to be the largest. Hence it was the first to be discerned – by Alfonso Marcue González in 1929 and by José Carlos Salinas Chávez in 1951. The latter thought it was Juan Diego, but according to specialists that was impossible, as Indians were not bearded. Charles Wahling put forward a different interpretation. He conjectured that the said man was the then newly-appointed general administrator of Mexico, the bishop of Santo Domingo, Ramírez y Fuenleal. According to historical documents, it appears that he was Bishop Juan de Zumárraga's guest on December 12, 1531.

José Aste Tonsmann also discovered a group of seven people at the central point of the image, in Mary's pupils. "It seems to be a family, parents and five children, but its identity is as yet unknown."[191]

Tonsmann believes that this "hidden" message is for "modern times when technology is able to discover it. 'This could be the case of the picture of the family in the center of the Virgin's eye,' he says, 'at a time when the family is under serious attack in our modern world.'"[192] Despite the uncertainty of the identity of the mystery family, Tonsmann noted with certainty that science is unable to explain how the reflections in the eyes came about. Still, some remained skeptical of Tonsmann's findings, most notably, Luis Martínez Negrete, a declared atheist and Tonsmann's former boss at IBM's scientific research center.

Consequently, in 2006, Fr. Eduardo Chávez Sanches and Fr. José Luis Guerrero Rosado, two canons from the Basilica of Our Lady of Guadalupe, invited Negrete to try to discredit the work of his former employee. As an avowed atheist, Negrete would have liked nothing more than to do just that. To his chagrin, however, he was unable to contradict any of Tonsmann's work and was forced to agree with all his former subordinate's conclusions.

The Peruvian researcher's revelations prompted further studies. Understanding that human vision is characteristic of certain principles of projection and reflection, Fernando Ojeda Llanes began his investigation into the degree in which the images reflected in the irises of the Virgin's two eyes are in harmony with those standards. His meticulous work in 2008 concluded that, "observing all the laws of optics – the images in both eyes showed a correspondence of 98.45 percent."[193] This is the singular most unique manifestation in the world. This image measures seventy-six inches by forty-one inches. Our Lady herself is fifty-six inches from head to foot, while the diameter of her irises is a mere 5/16 inch. It is understandable why the images in Mary's eyes remained undetected for over four hundred years. This further supports the revelation that the image is not a painting since no human could have painted an image in 1531 that observes near total conformity with the laws of optics, laws that were not even known for another four hundred years.

Part V

The Impact of
Our Lady of Guadalupe
on 21st Century Life

Chapter 16
Our Lady of Guadalupe,
The Mother of All Life

Our Lady appeared to Juan Diego to "offer faith, hope and consolation to the oppressed natives of Mexico and to reconcile them with their Spanish rulers."[194] Her appearance ended the bloody human sacrifice of the Aztecs and the imagery of her portrait was so powerful to the Aztec Indians that it was responsible for the conversion of some eight to nine million natives in the eight to ten-year period following the apparitions!

"To the extent that an icon expresses in color and form a mystic meaning, to that extent it is a great icon...If [the iconographer] is to express a mystery, an artist must be graced with contemplative insight...Now, the artist of the image of Our Lady of Guadalupe is none other than the Mother of God, and in it She shows Herself to be the 'icon painter' par excellence."[195]

So many aspects of the image spoke to the indigenous people. It is by all accounts an Aztec pictograph which they read and immediately understood. By standing in front of the sun, Our Lady acknowledged that She was far greater than Huitzilopochtli, the dreaded Aztec sun-god, and Her foot resting on the crescent moon made it clear that She had conquered Quetzalcoatl, their most notable deity. The aqua of Her mantle, a color reserved for royalty, signified that She was a Queen, and the stars that decorated the garment told the Aztecs that She was greater than the heavenly stars that they worshipped. The very placement of those stars on Her mantle held significance to the Aztecs. With the northern crown upon Her head and Virgo resting over Her womb, the very constellations that graced that early morning's sky adorned Her body. The black belt on her waist recalled the Aztec Maternity Belt and the four-petal flower over Her womb signified that this pregnant woman was the Mother of God, as "the flower was a special symbol of life, movement and deity – the center of the universe."[196] Her hands, joined in prayer, indicate that there was one greater than She and the brooch with the inlaid cross to which She points acknowledges that that someone is Her Son, Jesus The Christ. Finally, the design on Her rose-colored garment indicates that "She is the 'Queen of Earth,' for she is wearing a map of Mexico telling the Indians exactly where the apparition took place."[197]

Our Lady is not the Mother of only the Aztecs, however, and the symbolism contained within Her image spoke to the Catholic Spaniards as well. By positioning Herself on the moon and surrounding Herself with the sun's rays, Our Lady invoked the Christian Scriptures. The particular reference is found in St. John's Revelations, in which he wrote, "A great sign appeared in the sky, a woman clothed with the sun, with the moon under her feet, and on her head a crown of twelve stars. She was with child..."[198] The Christian iconographic interpretation of the cloak of the sun could represent either the Immaculate Conception or the Assumption. By appearing on December 9, however, the day in which the entire Church celebrated the feast of the Holy

Conception of Mary at that time,* Our Lady clearly identifies that She is the Immaculate Conception. While She identified Herself with words at Lourdes, She does so with imagery in Mexico.

The message of Guadalupe is equally important today as it was in 1531. As the Mother of Life, Our Lady of Guadalupe has become the patroness of the cause for life, and that cause, in these uncertain times when life is considered so expendable by so many, has never been more critical. Statistics show that in this country alone, since the 1973 US Supreme Court Decision in Roe v Wade, over 64 million** babies have been slaughtered by the bloodied instruments of abortion.

These abortions are brutal and torturously slow with each of the baby's limbs being torn off its torso individually while the baby agonizingly tries to escape the ravage brought on by the implements of the torture.

In 1973, when the highest court in the land made its momentous decision on the value of life, it did so with an uncertain science as to when life begins. Without knowing a clear answer to that all-important question, the court still limited the right of a woman to have an abortion to the first trimester of pregnancy and the nation's leading abortion service was quick to claim that all they wanted was to make the procedure legal, safe and rare.

NOTE: In 1531, the entire Church, both east and west, celebrated the Feast of the Immaculate Conception on the same day, December 9th. Today, the west celebrates that feast day on December 8th while the eastern Church continues to commemorate it on December 9th.

**NOTE: While exact figures are difficult to obtain because there are no consistent reporting methods for abortion, the Guttmacher Institute estimates that 52.6 million abortions were performed between 1973 and 2011, the most recent year for which data is available. Using that as the base and extrapolating it through 2019, it can be reasonably deduced that the number of abortions in the United States since the Roe v. Wade decision is over 64 million, though some estimate the number to be as high as 73 million.*

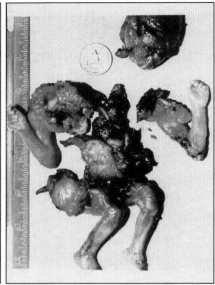

While the ancient sacrifice of human children is today viewed as horrific, government leaders and their supporters currently advocate for the horrible, inhumane execution of millions of babies who desperately fight the abortionists attempts to tear the baby's limbs from the torso.(Photos courtesy of Citizens for a pro-life society. www.prolifesociety.com)

Since that time, science has formalized the response to the question of when life begins, confirming that life begins at the moment of conception. There is no longer any debate that the zygote, the product of a fertilized egg, is in fact a human life. In the face of this revelation, those intent on the destruction of human life did not back down from legalized abortion, they doubled down. So, some forty-seven years following the Supreme Court's decision, proponents now consider abortion a guaranteed form of health care and euphemistically refer to the destruction of human life as reproductive health. Making abortion safe and rare is no longer the priority now that it is legal. In fact, a dearth of legislative reforms has swept the nation. These bills allow for abortion at any time, including up to the moment of birth, and an abortion is allowed pretty much for any reason. Many states, including New York, California, Rhode

Island, and a host of others, now argue that a so-called right to control one's own body is paramount to the life of an unborn child.

On June 21, 2019, Justice Nathalie Lievan, a judge in Britain's Court of Protection, took up the case of a mentally disabled Catholic woman who was ordered by a government agency to have an abortion against her will. Under Britain's government-controlled, single-payer health care system, such a recommendation can be made. Tests indicated that not withstanding the mother's mental status, the twenty-two-week-old fetus was not impaired and was, in fact, completely normal. In addition, the pregnant woman's mother and midwife said that they would care for the baby. None of that mattered to the judge. Fortunately, this decision was quickly

Our Lady told Juan Diego that She is the protector of life. Could She possibly watch idly as Her babies are slaughtered in abortion clinics by the millions? Since the passage of Roe v. Wade, conservative estimates place the number of abortions at 64 million. As this book is being printed, state houses around the nation are clamoring to pass legislation allowing for the slaughter of babies right up to the moment of birth and one state proposed infanticide.

overturned by a higher court. Regardless, it is a prime example of the little worth that society places on human life. Such a reckless attitude toward life is disturbing at best and damning at worst.

A nation like the United States that passes laws to protect wild-life at all stages of development (in the United States it is a crime to destroy the egg of an American Bald Eagle while in the State of Rhode Island it is a crime to destroy the egg of a piping plover), laws protecting human life are being relaxed. One US state even considered passage of a bill that would have legalized infanticide allowing a baby born alive to lay "comfortably" on the table while the mother and doctor discuss whether or not to allow the baby to continue to live.[199]

Today most people recoil in horror when stories are told of the Aztecs tying down their sacrificial victims and extracting the beating hearts from their chests. "But America is not doing any better, as the hearts and heads of innocent babies are destroyed by abortion!"[200] Just as the image of Our Lady was used in 1531 for the conversion of some nine million Aztec people, it is being used again today to change the hearts of our people. "A key theological dynamic operating here is that Our Lady turned the Aztecs from a worldview of despair to one of hope, from a conviction that the gods were against them to a conviction that God was so much *for* them that *He became one of them.*"[201]

Copies of the same image that converted so many Aztec Indians travels the United States on an unequivocal mission to end abortion. The image has been honored in many churches throughout the country and has been brought outside abortion clinics where faithful and ardent Catholics hold prayer vigils. And the results have been dramatic. In Florida, Helena, a Catholic girl who was already inside the waiting room of an abortion clinic peered out the window. A missionary image of Our Lady of Guadalupe caught her eye. She cancelled her abortion and those praying outside the clinic arranged for all the assistance she needed. Fr. Frank Pavone, the National Director of Priests for Life, who himself was one of the people praying when the girl left the clinic, baptized Helena's baby. Helena named her daughter Guadalupe.

The image of Our Lady of Guadalupe is miraculous and to this day is responsible for wondrous events. When the image was taken to an abortuary in Wichita, Kansas, where late-term abortions were being performed daily as the bodies were cremated on site, the fragrance of roses was detected as the image was processed around the center. Witnesses also observed rose petals falling from the image in all directions.

When the image was displayed in a public park, Vicki, a pregnant mother happened by. She already made the decision to abort her baby but when she peered at the image of Our Lady, "her knees began to shake, and she spontaneously began to cry. 'When I saw the Missionary image, it was like the Holy Spirit was coming into me and waking me up after many years,'"[202] Vicki said. Vicki had never heard of Our Lady of Guadalupe, but still heard an inner voice tell her that she was called to motherhood. She decided against killing her baby and gave birth to a healthy baby boy. In addition, she abandoned the "New Age" movement that she had been attracted to and returned to the sacraments after a number of years away. She now dedicates her life to helping mothers and their unborn children. Similar stories abound and prove the point that Our Lady is still using Her image of Guadalupe, not only to save lives, but as a means of conversion as well.

According to Fr. Pavone, "the image speaks to these girls a message of hope. It also speaks to the pro-life people a message about the task before us. We who fight abortion do not see abortion walking down the street. Instead, we see a girl, frightened and in the grip of despair. We, the Church, are to reach out to her in what is the most critical pastoral mission of our day.

Our Lady of Guadalupe has been declared the 'Patroness of the unborn.' They will be saved by the message of hope She brings, and by the message of concrete charity with which She challenges the Church."[203]

Chapter 17
The Knights of Columbus and Our Lady of Guadalupe

In 1882 Father Michael J. McGivney, looking for a way to provide care to widows and orphans of his parish in New Haven, Connecticut, met with a group of men in the basement of St. Mary's Church. From that inauspicious meeting, the Knights of Columbus was founded. Over the course of the next 137 years the organization has grown into a worldwide network of almost two million Catholic men scattered throughout the United States, Canada, Mexico, the Philippines, the Caribbean, Central America, and other nations. As a body, The Knights are "dedicated to upholding the moral teachings of the Catholic Church and the order's core principles of Charity, Unity, Fraternity, and Patriotism. They have also become an effective advocate and defender of civil and religious rights for all."[204]

In 1882, Fr. Michael J. McGivney established the Knights of Columbus, a fraternal organization dedicated to Our Lady. Over the years the Knights have worked indefatigably to protect life at all stages. The Knights obviously have a special devotion to Our Lady of Guadalupe.

Now with over fourteen thousand councils, the Knights of Columbus has become the world's largest Catholic fraternal organization. They are inspired by the growing list of their members who have become saints, including six Mexican members who were martyred in the 1920s.

A defining characteristic of the Knights of Columbus is the deep devotion of its members to the Blessed Virgin. Upon becoming a Knight, each member is given a Rosary and encouraged to regard Mary as his own Mother so that through Her, he may grow closer to Her Son Jesus. The two titles of Mary under which the Knights are especially devoted are the Immaculate Conception and Our Lady of Guadalupe, the Patronesses of the Americas, though the Knights have always been apostles of the Rosary and have undertaken countless Marian initiatives over the years.

In 1905, Supreme Knight Edward L. Hearn established the Guadalupe Council of the Knights while visiting Mexico City. It was the first council of Knights established in Mexico. Since that time, the Knights worldwide have had a special devotion of Our Lady of Guadalupe sponsoring and promoting events all over the globe in honor of the Patroness of the Americas.

During his visit to the Our Lady of Guadalupe Basilica in 2000, Supreme Knight Carl Anderson dedicated his administration to Her. Consequently, in the United States, the organization cosponsored the 2003 "tilma of Tepeyac Tour" in which Knights carried "the relic of the tilma from the Cathedral in Los Angeles to more than twenty cities in the United States, drawing in excess of one hundred thousand people."[205]

In 2007, the Knights commemorated the 475th anniversary of Our Lady of Guadalupe by sponsoring a speaking tour featuring Guadalupan expert Msgr. Eduardo Chávez who also served as the postulator for the cause of canonization of St. Juan Diego. The Knights served as host to the first of its kind International Marian Congress on Our Lady of Guadalupe in 2009, an event that "concluded with the 22,000-person Guadalupe Festival in Phoenix, Arizona."[206] Also in that year, Supreme Knight Anderson, along with Msgr. Eduardo Chávez, co-authored New York Times best-selling book *Our Lady of Guadalupe: Mother of a Civilization of Love.*

In 2010, the Order sponsored the Rosary of Guadalupan Love at the Mexico City Basilica and in 2011, a Marian Prayer Program dedicated to Our Lady of Guadalupe was launched for the fourth time. The Knights' Marian Prayer Program has spread devotion of Our Lady of Guadalupe to parishes throughout the world.

The Knights of Columbus Silver Rose program is another way in which the Knights bring honor to Our Lady of Guadalupe and promote the cause of life. The Silver Rose is a dedication to St. Juan Diego and his meeting with Our Lady as it commemorates the Miracle of the Roses. It was when Juan Diego unfurled the tilma in which he carried the flowers, that the image of Our Lady of Guadalupe appeared on the cactus-fiber.

Some Knights believe that this program is the perfect way for the organization to "not only honor Our Lady but reaffirm our dedication to the sanctity of human life." Brother Robert Julien believes the One Life, One Rose program is "now a pro-life emblem as well because of the culture of very radically available abortions."[207] It is hoped by the Knights that simply seeing the rose will prompt people to pray for an end to abortion.

Conclusion

Located in Mexico City, not far from the Basilica of Our Lady of Guadalupe, is a scientific research center dedicated to the exploration of the unique phenomena associated with the image of Our Lady on the tilma of Juan Diego. The Higher Institute for Guadalupan Studies (*Instituto Superior de Estudios Guadalupanos – ISEG*) was established in 1998 and is inextricably linked to the cause of sainthood for Juan Diego. Some in the press, supported by others in the clergy however, denied the very existence of Juan Diego noting that he was a mythological character created in the imagination of zealots. The claims led to the creation of a special historical commission, established by the Church within the Center, to scrutinize the alleged uncertainties.

The commission included three eminent Mexican historians; Fr. Fidel González Fernandez, Fr. José Luis Guerrero Rosado, and Fr. Eduardo Chávez Sánchez. In 2001, after three years of tedious research, the Commission concluded "that Diego's existence was without doubt a historical fact."[208] Only then did Pope John Paul II consider the canonization of Juan Diego, which occurred on July 31, 2002.

The attacks by the secular media and others did not end with the commission's conclusions, however, and by 2003, there were still many myths and misrepresentations circulating about the image of Our Lady of Guadalupe. In response, Norberto Cardinal Rivera Carrera decided the time was right to establish a center dedicated to scientific research focusing on the phenomena associated with the image. That was the birth of ISEG. The Center enjoys the support and work of many historians, archeologists, ethnographers, mathematicians, astronomers, and ophthalmologists. It highlights new discoveries, organizes a number of international congresses and sponsors seminars. ISEG is also involved in the production of films and the issuance of publications all under the direction of Fr. Eduardo Chávez Sánchez, the most widely acclaimed expert of all things Guadalupan.

Since the appearance of the image of Our Lady of Guadalupe on the tilma of Juan Diego in 1531, it has been the object of veneration, study, scientific analysis, marvel and, of course, ridicule by disbelievers who try to discredit its authenticity. Yet nothing, not even the most modern and sophisticated equipment known to science, can explain the miraculous nature of the image which has been manifested in a variety of ways.

The mere number of conversions that have been attributed to the image of Our Lady on the tilma is in itself miraculous, especially considering the very limited success of the trained missionaries of the Dominican, Franciscan, and Augustinian Orders. Their efforts resulted in the conversion of approximately one million people between 1521 and 1531 when Our Lady appeared to Juan Diego. Yet, in the ten-year period post-apparition, that number jumped to over nine million and included some of the most savage native Indians known to Mexico at the time.

The very nature of the image is miraculous. Initially thought to be paint on a cheap, untreated cloth, science, to its amazement, has discovered that the image actually had the properties of a photograph, not a painting, despite being generated some three hundred years before the invention of photography.

Another miraculous feature about the image on the tilma is its indestructible nature despite the many intentional and unintentional occasions it has had to suffer destruction. The material of which the tilma is made is the cheapest of cactus fibers with an expected life of no more than forty or fifty years, especially when one considers the extreme abuse, both environmental and physical to which the tilma has been exposed. Despite exposure to the salinity of the air, smoke and heat of candles, the accidental acid spill, the innumerable hands and objects that have held it or been held to it, and the intentional bomb blast in 1921, the cloth has survived in pristine condition and the colors of the tilma are as sharp today as they were in 1531. Even the very imperfections of the cloth were used by Our Lady to provide a 3-D effect to the image.

The reflection of thirteen additional people in the eyes of the Virgin could not have been painted and, though appearing over four hundred years before the ophthalmological principles of modern optometry and ophthalmology were known, the image on the tilma conforms to all of them. Of course, throughout these studies many ophthalmologists, who looked into the eyes of Mary on the tilma with modern equipment, noted how they had the sensation of peering into living eyes, not the eyes of someone pictured on a photograph.

The alignment of the stars on the tilma are reflective of the sky over Mexico City on the exact day, and at the exact time, at which the image was revealed to Bishop Zumárraga and his cohorts, by Juan Diego. And, because Juan Diego revealed the image at the exact time that he did, the constellation comprised of the stars on Mary's mantle are exactly where they need to be on Her body to conform to Biblical prophecy.

The mathematical findings regarding the conformance of the flowers with the mountains and volcanos, and the production of a perfectly harmonious melody when the stars are placed on a musical scale, all point to inexplicable miracles in the creation of one of the world's most significant portraits.

All of these findings are enigma and none of them can be explained by science. Yet no one has been able to successfully dispute the existence of any of them. Considering the rapid advances being made in technology, it is reasonable to expect that as scientific techniques advance further, more discoveries will be made that will shed additional light on the miraculous nature of the amazing "selfie" left on the tilma by Our Lady of Guadalupe. To that point, Fr. Eduardo Chávez Sánchez notes that "science has not as yet said its last word concerning the enigmatic elements of the extraordinary image, such as the amazing discoveries concerning Our Lady's eyes."[209]

Chronology of Events

(Sources include Guadalupe Mysteries: Deciphering the Code *by Grzegorz Gorny and Janusz Rosikon: and* The Miracle Hunter Marian Apparitions: Guadalupe – *Michael O'Neill)*

1325: The creation of the first settlement of Aztecs on an island in Lake Texcoco. There they spotted an eagle perched on a cactus and devouring a snake, something they took as a sign of destiny. Today that image adorns the flag of Mexico.

1474: Cuauhtlatoa (later kniown as – Juan Diego) is born in Cuautitlán, Mesoamerica (now Mexico).

1476: Juan de Zumárraga is born in Spain.

1492: Italian born Christopher Columbus, sailing for the Spanish Crown, discovers the Americas.

1505: The Aztecs elect Moctezuma II their Emperor.

1514: The city of Higuey establishes the first Marian Shrine in the New World.

1519: Hernán Cortés lands in Mesoamerica (Mexico) as a conqueror for the Spanish Crown.

1520: Moctezuma is deposed and dies. The new Emperor temporarily drives out the Spaniards.

1521: Cortés conquers the Mesoamerican capital city of Tenochtitlan.

1524: The first twelve Franciscan missionaries arrive in Mexico.

1525: Quauhtiatoatzin is baptized by a Franciscan priest and receives the Christian name of Juan Diego.

1527: Cuautlatoa is baptized into the Catholic faith. His wife María Lucia is also baptized.

1528: Juan de Zumárraga, a Franciscan Friar from Spain, arrives in Mesoamerica and becomes known as the protector of the Indians.

1529: Juan Diego's wife María dies.

Dec. 9, 1531: The Virgin Mother of God appears to Juan Diego on top of Tepeyac Hill speaking to him in his native language of Nahuatl. She requests that he go to the bishop of Mexico and petition him to "build me a temple right here" (teocalli). Juan Diego agrees to carry out her wishes and meets with the bishop. Though cordial, the bishop does not believe him. On his return home, Juan Diego meets the Virgin again and She tells him to return to the bishop the next day with the same message and request.

Dec. 10, 1531: Juan Diego meets with the bishop a second time. The bishop patiently listened but, before agreeing to build a church, asked Juan to get him a sign to prove that the Lady was really the Mother of God. On the way home, Mary appeared to Juan again and promised that She would provide the requested sign the following day. Juan stops to visit his uncle, Juan Bernardino, and finds him very sick.

Dec. 11, 1531: Juan Diego misses his appointment with the Lady so that he could stay home and take care of his uncle who is clearly dying. Juan Bernardino begs Juan Diego to go get a priest from the church in Tlaltelolco so he can make his last confession. As it was already very late, Juan promises his uncle that he will do so the following morning.

Dec. 12, 1531: Juan Diego takes a slightly different route to avoid the delay of meeting with Our Lady. Regardless, Juan still encounters Mary who promised that his uncle was already healed and is no longer in need of a priest. She instructs him instead to climb Tepeyac Hill to gather the flowers growing there in winter as the sign that the bishop requested. He does so, placing the flowers in his tilma which he presents to Mary. Our Lady rearranges the flowers in Juan's tilma, and he departs to meet the bishop. As Juan unfurls his tilma before the bishop, a portrait of Our Lady appears.

Dec. 13, 1531: Juan Diego, at the bishop's request, shows him the exact site of the apparitions. Then he and the bishop's men go to the house of Uncle Juan Bernardino and find him healed just as Mary promised. Bernardino reports that he too received a visit from the Virgin who identified herself as what the bishop's men understand to be Our Lady of Guadalupe.

Dec. 24, 1531: Bishop Zumárraga writes a letter to Hernán Cortés in which he acknowledges that "I want to dedicate my cathedral to the Immaculate Conception because it was during that feast that God and his Blessed Mother deigned to shower the land you won with great favor.

Dec. 26, 1531: The image of Our Lady of Guadalupe is transferred to the sanctuary of the newly completed, one-room chapel (the first chapel). While festivities were still underway, an Indian is accidently shot in the neck with an arrow. He is taken to the chapel where the others pray for the intervention of Our Lady of

Guadalupe. The Indian regains his life. This is proclaimed the first miracle associated with the image.

1533: A larger adobe chapel is erected at the site of the apparition (the second chapel). The bishop gives Juan Diego permission to move into a room that was added to the back of the chapel. He remains there for the balance of his life. The miraculous image is placed in the small church and was venerated by many pilgrims.

1544: The Cocollizti Plague kills about 12,000 Indians in Mexico City alone, but the disease stops after the Franciscan missionaries lead children, six and seven years old, to the shrine to pray.

1545: Don Antonio Valeriano writes the Nican Mopohua between 1540 – 1545: It is the earliest surviving account of the apparitions.

1548: Bishop Juan de Zumárraga dies. Juan Diego also dies and is buried in the first chapel dedicated to the Virgin of Guadalupe. The Codex is written. It is the first document that commemorates Juan Diego's death, provides an illustration of him and makes the earliest reference to his Indian name.

1555: Alonso de Montúfar, the second archbishop of Mexico, formulates canons that indirectly approved the apparitions.

1556: Archbishop Montúfar begins construction of the third (sometimes referred to as the second) church at the site of the apparitions. It has become known as the Old Church of the Indians.

1551 – 1561: The Nican Mopohua is written by an Indian by the name of Antonio Valeriano.

1567: The new church ordered by Archbishop Montúfar is complete.

1570: Archbishop Montúfar sends an oil-painted copy of the image of the Virgin of Guadalupe to Spain's King Phillip II.

1571: Admiral Andrea Doria carries a copy of the image aboard his ship during the battle of Lepanto and attributes the victory over the Ottoman Empire to the Virgin of Guadalupe.

1573: Historian Juan de Tovar writes the "Primitive Source," a book he transcribed from an earlier source probably written by Juan González, Bishop Zumárraga's translator.

Sept 21, 1629: The flood that killed 30,000 Indians and 20,000 Spaniards in Mexico City begins. An additional 27,000 Indians flee, leaving only 400 city inhabitants. The Sacred image is removed by boat and taken to the Cathedral.

1633: The first synthetic studies of the tilma are performed by a group of physicians and painters. Prof. Tanco Becerra signed the final report of the group's behalf. The report of the thirteen-year study drew attention to the diffraction effect on the material.

May 14, 1634: The image of Our Lady of Guadalupe is returned to Tepeyac in grand procession. The flood waters remained for over four years.

1647: The image of Our Lady of Guadalupe is covered with glass for the first time.

1648: Fr. Miguel Sánchez publishes "Image of the Virgin Mary, Guadalupan Mother of God" in Mexico City.

1647 – 1649: Bachiller Luis Lasso de la Vega publishes the *"Huei Tlama Huizoltica"* (The Story of the Miracle of Guadalupe) copied from Don Antonio Valeriano's *Nican Mopohua*. It tells the story in the language of Nahuatl.

1666: The Catholic Church conducts the Informaciones Guadalupana, a formal inquiry into the apparitions and calls Juan Diego a "holy man." The inquiry lasted from February 18th to March 22nd.

1666: A chapel is built on Tepeyac Hill, the site of the first apparition of Our Lady of Guadalupe to Juan Diego, the spot where the flowers were picked on December 12, 1531.

1695: Construction of the Sanctuary dedicated to Our Lady of Guadalupe is begun with the laying of the first stone.

April 27, 1709: The new sanctuary is dedicated in solemn ceremony.

1723: Archbishop Lanziego y Equilaz orders a second formal investigation of the apparitions of Our Lady of Guadalupe.

1736: The Plague, either cocollixti or typhus, resurfaces, killing seven hundred thousand people. In Mexico City alone, 40,000 die.

1737: Mexico chooses the Most Holy Mary of Guadalupe as its patroness.

1746: All of New Spain accepts the patronage of Our Lady of Guadalupe while Knight Boturini Benaducci promotes the official coronation of the image.

1751: Miguel Cabrera led a group of Mexican painters in an effort to determine the technique that was used to produce the image. After an exhaustive five-year study that ended in 1756, they were unable to do so.

May 25, 1754: Pope Benedict XIV approves the patronage of New Spain and declares December 12 a day of liturgical celebration.

1756: Painter Miguel Cabrera publishes his book, "American Marvel," in which he releases the result of his extensive study of the image.

1767: The Spanish Dominions expel the Religious Society of Jesus who then carry the image to various parts of the world.

1785: A chapel worker cleaning the case in which the tilma was displayed accidently spilled a 50% nitric acid solution directly on the image on the tilma. Miraculously, the image was not damaged.

1789: The results of an experiment conducted by Mexican Mathematician Dr. José Ignacio Bartolache were published. The result confirmed the unparalleled durability of the agave material of which the tilma was composed.

1810: Father Miguel Hidalgo creates a battle flag using Our Lady of Guadalupe at the start of the Mexican War of Independence from Spain.

Mar. 12, 1887: Pope Leo XIII orders the crowning of the Image of Our Lady of Guadalupe.

1894: Pope Leo XIII approves a new Office and Mass of Our Lady of Guadalupe.

Oct. 12, 1895: The coronation of the image is performed. It is attended by much of the episcopate of the Americas.

1910: Pope Pius X declares Our Lady of Guadalupe the Patroness of Latin America.

1911: The site of Juan Bernardino's home is used to build a church.

1921: Luciano Perez Carpio tries to destroy the image of Our Lady of Guadalupe by planting a vase of flowers with twenty-nine sticks of dynamite on the altar directly beneath it. Despite massive destruction of the church, the tilma is not damaged.

1924: Anthropologist M. H. Saville finds in Tetliapalco, Peru, the Codex Saville-Tetliapalco, a most important 16th-century source documenting the miracle. It is pictorial calendar that shows the image of Our Lady located in the position representing the year 1531.

1928: Santa Fe, Argentina coronates the image.

1929: Mexican photographer Alfonso Marcue Gonzales becomes the first person to discover an image, that of a bearded man, in the eyes of the Madonna of Guadalupe.

Dec. 10, 1933: Our Lady of Guadalupe is crowned in Rome. Two days later a Pontifical Mass was said in St. Peter's. Pope Pius XI proclaims Her patronage over Latin America repeating what Pope Pius X declared in 1910.

1935: Pope Pius XI extends the patronage of Our Lady of Guadalupe to the Philippines.

1936: German Chemist Richard Kuhn, a Nobel Prize winning chemist, was unable to identify the dye on the fibers of the image.

Dec. 12, 1950: Construction begins on the Plaza of the Americas. It is inaugurated on November 25. The structure, built on land donated by the Mexican government, faces the Basilica.

1951: The tilma is examined by Mexican photographer Carlos Salinas, who observes the apparent reflection of a man's head in the right eye of the Virgin when studying an enlargement of a photograph.

1956: Dr. Javier Torroella Bueno, a Mexican ophthalmologist, uses a magnifying glass to examine the eyes of the image on the tilma and confirms the discoveries of Marcue Gonzales and Salinas Chávez.

1957: Using an Ophthalmoscope, Mexican ophthalmologist Dr. Rafael Torija Lavoignet, examined the eyes of the image, discovering the stereoscopic effect.

1958: Dr. Rafael Torija Lavoignet publishes his study of the Purkinje-Sanson effect as exhibited in the eyes of the image.

1961: Pope John XXIII prays to Our Lady of Guadalupe as the Mother of the Americas.

1962: American ophthalmologist Charles Wahlig and his wife Isabelle Wahlig, an optician, enlarge the image of Our Lady of Guadalupe twenty-five times and discover two new reflections in the irises of the Virgin.

1962: The boulevard (Calzada de los Misterios) which covers the original road on which Juan Diego walked from Tepeyac to the Bishop's residence, is restored by the government.

1975: Dr. Enrique Grave, an ophthalmologist, is allowed to examine the image outside of its protective glass.

1976: The new Basilica of Our Lady of Guadalupe is dedicated. It is located four miles from Central Mexico. The image of Our Lady of Guadalupe is transferred from the old Basilica.

1979: American biophysicist Dr. Philip S. Callahan uses infra-red photography to take forty frames of photographs of the image. After an extensive study of the photographs, he concludes that the image is unexplainable as a work of human hands, as there are no signs of the use of a paintbrush.

That same year, José Aste Tonsmann, a Peruvian engineer, used computer enhancement techniques to enlarge the eyes of the image by 2,500 times. He discovers a group of thirteen people reflected in the eye of Our Lady.

Pope John Paul II knelt before the image of Our Lady of Guadalupe referring to Her as the "Star of Evangelization" and invoking Her motherly assistance. He called upon Her as the Mother of the Americas.

Dec. 22, 1981: Mexican astronomer Dr. Juan Rovero Hernán de Illescas demonstrated that the arrangement of the stars on Mary's mantle on the image resembled the one that was to be found over the sky in Mexico at the exact time that Juan Diego unfurled his tilma before Bishop Zumárraga. Further, the star map on the tilma is in the reverse providing a view of the constellations as seen from the heavens rather than from the earth.

1987: Juan Diego is declared venerable by the Congregation for the Causes of Saints.

1988: Fr. Mario Rojas Sánchez initiated a new way of examining the image by placing a map of Mexico on Mary's image. In so doing, he discovered a conformity of iconographic and geographic elements.
The celebration of Our Lady of Guadalupe on December 12 is elevated to the status of a feast in all dioceses in the United States.

May 6, 1990: Pope John Paul II beatifies Juan Diego in the Basilica of Santa María de Guadalupe in Mexico City, declaring December 9 his feast day and also invoking him as the protector and advocate of indigenous people.

1992: Pope John Paul II dedicates a chapel in honor of Our Lady of Guadalupe in St. Peter's Basilica.

1995: The Codex 1548, also known as Codex Escalada, commemorating the death of Juan Diego in 1548, is discovered in a private collection.

1996: Fr. William Schulenburg[210], a longtime abbot of the Basilica of Our Lady of Guadalupe, sparks controversy when he calls Juan Diego a mythical character.

July 31, 1997: Fr. Xavier Escalada, S.J., publishes an illustration of the apparition with the signature of Don Antonio Valeriano dated 1548 from the Codex stating that the Codex was scientifically studied and determined to be genuine.

1998: The Vatican establishes a commission of thirty researchers from various countries to study the question of the historical authenticity of Juan Diego. The research produced a death certificate of Juan Diego and concluded that he had indeed existed.

Fr. Mario Rojas Sánchez developed a new way to examine the image of Our Lady of Guadalupe by placing a map of Mexico on Mary's image. He discovered a conformity of iconographic and geographic elements.

Mar. 25, 1999: Pope John Paul II, declares the date of December 12 as a Liturgical Holy Day for the entire continent.

July 31, 2002: Juan Diego is canonized a saint by Pope John Paul II in Mexico City

2003: The Higher Institute for Guadalupan Studies is established in Mexico City, Mexico and historian, Fr. Eduardo Chávez Sánchez, is named its executive director. The institute is tasked with exploring the scientific phenomena connected with the image.

2006: Mexican engineer Luis Martínez Negrete confirms José Aste Tonsmann's revelation regarding the group of thirteen people reflected in the eye of Our Lady.

Dec. 12, 2011: Pope Benedict XVI stated:

The venerated image of the Black Madonna of Tepeyac, with Her sweet and peaceful countenance, imprinted on the tilma of the Indian St. Juan Diego, shows Her as "the ever-Virgin Mary, Mother of the True God from whom she lives." (From the Office of Readings. Nican Mopohua, 12th ed., Mexico City, D.F. 1971, 3-19) She reminds us of the "woman clothed with the sun, with the moon under Her feet, and on Her head a crown of twelve stars. She was with child." (Rev 12:1-2) She signals the presence of the Savior to the indigenous and mestizo population. She always leads us to Her divine Son, who is revealed as the foundation of the dignity of every human being, as a love that is stronger than the powers of evil and death, and the fountain of joy, filial trust, consolation and hope.

Prayers and Devotions to Our Lady of Guadalupe

Novena

Opening Prayer

Remember, O most gracious Virgin of Guadalupe, that in your heavenly apparitions on the mount of Tepeyac, you promised to show your compassion and pity towards all who, loving and trusting you, seek your help and call upon you in their necessities and afflictions. You promised to hear our supplications, to dry our tears, and to give us consolation and relief.

Never has it been known that anyone who fled to your protection, implored your help, or sought your intercession, was left unaided. Inspired by this confidence, we fly to you, O Mary, ever-Virgin Mother of the true God! Though grieving under the weight of our sins, we come to prostrate ourselves before you. We fully trust that, standing beneath your shadow and protection, nothing will trouble or afflict us, nor do we need to fear illness or misfortune, or any other sorrow.

O Virgin of Guadalupe, you want to remain with us through your admirable Image, you who are our Mother, our health, and our life. Placing ourselves beneath your maternal gaze, and having recourse to you in all our necessities, we need do nothing more.

O Holy Mother of God, despise not our petitions, but in your mercy hear and answer us. Amen.

Novena Daily Prayers (to be said following the Opening Prayer)

Day 1: Dearest Lady of Guadalupe, fruitful Mother of holiness, teach me your ways of gentleness and strength. Hear my humble prayer offered with heartfelt confidence to beg this favor (mention your intention here).

Day 2: O Mary, conceived without sin, I come to your throne of grace to share the fervent devotion of your faithful Mexican children who call to you under the glorious Aztec title of Guadalupe. Obtain for me a lively faith to do your Son's holy will always: May His will be done on earth as it is in heaven.

Day 3: O Mary, whose Immaculate Heart was pierced by seven swords of grief, help me to walk valiantly amid the sharp thorns strewn across my pathway. Obtain for me the strength to be a true imitator of you. This I ask you, my dear Mother.

Day 4: Dearest Mother of Guadalupe, I beg you for a fortified will to imitate your divine Son's charity, to always seek the good of others in need. Grant me this, I humbly ask of you.

Day 5: O most holy Mother, I beg you to obtain for me pardon of all my sins, abundant graces to serve your Son more faithfully from now on, and lastly, the grace to praise Him with you forever in heaven.

Day 6: Mary, Mother of vocations, multiply priestly vocations and fill the earth with religious houses which will be light and warmth for the world, safety in stormy nights. Beg your Son to send us many priests and religious. This we ask of you, O Mother.

Day 7: O Lady of Guadalupe, we beg you that parents live a holy life and educate their children in a Christian manner; that children obey and follow the directions of their parents; that all members of the family pray and worship together. This we ask of you, O Mother.

Day 8: With my heart full of the most sincere veneration, I prostrate myself before you, O Mother, to ask you to obtain for me the grace to fulfill the duties of my state in life with faithfulness and constancy.

Day 9: O God, You have been pleased to bestow upon us unceasing favors by having placed us under the special protection of the Most Blessed Virgin Mary. Grant us, your humble servants, who rejoice in honoring her today upon earth, the happiness of seeing her face to face in heaven.

Concluding Prayer

Our Father
Hail Mary
Glory Be

Pope Saint John Paul II's Prayer to Our Lady of Guadalupe

O Immaculate Virgin, Mother of the true God and Mother of the Church!, who from this place reveal your clemency and your pity to all those who ask for your protection, hear the prayer that we address to you with filial trust, and present it to your Son Jesus, our sole Redeemer.

Mother of Mercy, Teacher of hidden and silent sacrifice, to you, who come to meet us sinners, we dedicate on this day all our being and all our love. We also dedicate to you our life, our work, our joys, our infirmities and our sorrows. Grant peace, justice and prosperity to our peoples; for we entrust to your care all that we have and all that we are, our Lady and Mother. We wish to be entirely yours and to walk with you along the way of complete faithfulness to Jesus Christ in His Church; hold us always with your loving hand.

Virgin of Guadalupe, Mother of the Americas, we pray to you for all the Bishops, that they may lead the faithful along paths of intense Christian life, of love and humble service of God and souls. Contemplate this immense harvest, and intercede with the Lord that He may instill a hunger for holiness in the whole people of God, and grant abundant vocations of priests and religious, strong in the faith and zealous dispensers of God's mysteries.

Grant to our homes the grace of loving and respecting life in its beginnings, with the same love with which you conceived in your womb the life of the Son of God. Blessed Virgin Mary, protect our families, so that they may always be united, and bless the upbringing of our children.
Our hope, look upon us with compassion, teach us to go continually to Jesus and, if we fall, help us to rise again, to return to

Him, by means of the confession of our faults and sins in the Sacrament of Penance, which gives peace to the soul.

We beg you to grant us a great love for all the holy Sacraments, which are, as it were, the signs that your Son left us on earth.

Thus, Most Holy Mother, with the peace of God in our conscience, with our hearts free from evil and hatred, we will be able to bring to all true joy and true peace, which come to us from your son, our Lord Jesus Christ, who with God the Father and the Holy Spirit, lives and reigns for ever and ever.

Amen.

His Holiness John Paul II

Mexico, January 1979. Visiting Her Basilica during his first foreign trip as Pope.

Bibliography

Books:

Bancroft, Hubert Howe. Volume X History of Mexico Vol II 1521-1600. San Francisco: A.L. Bancroft and Company, 1883.

Chávez, Eduardo, Our Lady of Guadalupe and Saint Juan Diego: The Historical Evidence. Translated from Spanish by Carmen Trevino and Veronica Montaño, Lanham, Boulder, New York, Toronto & Oxford, 2006.

Cortés, Hernán, Letters, (2005) [1523]. Cartas de relacion. Mexico: Editorial Porrua. (English translation).

Elizondo, Virgil, Guadalupe: Mother of the New Creation, New York: Orbis Books, 1997.

Gorny, Grzegorz and Rosikon, Janusz. Guadalupe Mysteries: Deciphering the Code, Ignatius Press, San Francisco and Rosikon Press, Warsaw, 2016.

Garibay, Angel M. Monsignor, A Handbook on Guadalupe, "The Spiritual Motherhood of Mary," Franciscan Friars of the Immaculate, Massachusetts 1996.

Johnston, Francis, The Wonder of Guadalupe, North Carolina: Tan Books, 2011.

Lawrence, C.H., The Friars – The Impact of the Early Mendicant Movement on Western Society., London & New York: Longman 1994.

The New American Bible, Translated from the Original Languages with Critical Use of All the Ancient Sources, Oxford Press, New York, 2011.

Wood, Stephanie, Transcending Conquest: Nahua Views of Spanish Colonial Mexico, Oklahoma University Press, Oklahoma, 2003.

Periodicals, Collections & Academic Studies:
De Sanctis, Dona, Ph. D., Columbus: Fact vs. Fiction, A Report from The Order Sons of Italy in America and The Commission for Social Justice. 2002, expanded October 2005.

Díaz del Catillo, Bernal. Historia verdadera de la conquista de la Nueva España. Colección Autral, Espasa-Calpe, 3rd Ed., Madrid 1975.

Dovas, Alexia, Why did the Aztecs Convert to Catholicism Following the Conquest of the Spaniards in 1521. Adelphia University – Nu of New York. Lambda Alpha Journal, Volume 37, 2007.

Foo, Lam Pin, How Mexico Was Conquered and Converted to Christianity. https://lampinfoo.com/2008/12/31/how-mexico-was-conquered-and-converted-to-christianity, December, 2008.

Landa, Fray Diego de, *Relacion de las cosas de Yucatán*, (Relationship of the Yucatán things) Colección Cronicas de America, Dastin, Madrid 2002. (Available on-line in Spanish as a PDF file on the website of the European Association of Mayanists.)

Waldinger, María, Colonial Missionaries and Long Run Development in Mexico, London School of Economics, May 2013.

Internet Sources:
Lynch, Dan, The Amazing Truth of Our Lady of Guadalupe, Catholic Exchange, December 2002. www.catholiceducation.org/en/culture/catholic-contributions/the-amazing-truth-of-our-lady-of-guadalupe-html.

Bouquet of Hatred at Guadalupe, http://www.catholickingdom.com/people/dominique/archive/inline/ff_131.html,

Castellano, Daniel J., Historiography of the Apparition of Guadalupe, Parts I-XIV. http://www.arcaneknowledge.org/catholic/guadalupe13.htm.

Catholic Online, St. Juan Diego, https://www.catholic.org/saints/saint.php?saint_id=73.

Catholic Sun, The, Karen, Knights Silver Rose Promotes Our Lady of Guadalupe, Respect for Human Life, As It Passes Through Diocese, Anthem, AZ.

https://catholicsun.org/2016/10/29/knights-silver-rose-promotes-our-lady-of-guadalupe.

Epic World History, Franciscans in the Americas, http://epic-worldhistory.blogspot.com/2012/06/franciscans-in-americas.html.

Hernán dez, Bernat, History Magazine, The Cortés Conquest, http://www.nationalgeographic.com/archeology-and-history/magazine/2016/05-06/Cortés-tenochtitlan. December 2018.

Klein, Christopher, The Viking Explorer Who Beat Columbus to America. htpps://www.history.com/news/the-viking-explorer-who-beat-columbus-to-america. October 2013.

Knights of Columbus, Our Lady of Guadalupe, 2018-2019, http://www.guadalupebook.com/gb/en/other/kofc_page.html

Latino Book Review, First Printing Press in the Americas was Established in Mexico, https//www.latinobookreview.com/first-printing-press-in-the-americas-was-established-in-mexico.html.

McRoskey, Ricky, The Bomb in the Basilica, https://www.catholicbusinessjournal.com/columns/ricky-mcroskey/the-bomb-in-the-basilica. December 12, 2018.

Our Lady of Guadalupe, Patroness of the Americas – Website. The Mystery in Our Lady's Eyes, https://www.sancta.org/eyes.html.

Pavone, Fr. Frank, Our Lady of Guadalupe and the Pro-life Movement, Priests for Life Website, Educational Resources. https//www.priestsforlife.org/articles/2791-our-lady-of-guadalupe-and-the-pro-life-movement.

Sewell, Matthew, 4 Literally Awesome Facts About Our Lady of Guadalupe, Mountain Catholic, https://mtncatholic.com/2014/12/11/4-literally-awesome-facts-about-our-lady-of-guadalupe/, December 11, 2014.

Wikipedia, Human Sacrifice in the Aztec Culture, https::en.wikipedia.org/wiki/human_sacrifice_in_Aztec_culture.

Wikipedia, Plutarco Elías Calles, https://en.wikipedia.org/wiki/Plutarco_El%C3%ADas_Calles.

This Day in History, Aztecs, https://www.history.com/topics/ancient-americas/aztecs.

Zenit Staff, Science Stunned by Virgin of Guadalupe's Eyes: Engineer Sees a Reflection, Literally, From a Scene in 1531. https://zenit.org/articles/science-stunned-by-virgin-of-guadalupe-s-eyes/. Rome, January 14, 2001.

Notes

[1] Johnston, Francis, The Wonder of Guadalupe, Tan Books, North Carolina 2011. Page 129.

[2] McRoskey, Ricky, The Bomb in the Basilica, https://www.catholicbusinessjournal.com/columns/ricky-mcroskey/the-bomb-in-the-basilica, Page 2.

[3] Foo, Lam Pin, How Mexico Was Conquered and Converted to Christianity. https://lampinfoo.com/2008/12/31/how-mexico-was-conquered-and-converted-to-christianity, December, 2008.

[4] This Day in History, Aztecs, https://www.history.com/topics/ancient-americas/aztecs.

[5] Human Sacrifice in the Aztec Culture, https::en.wikipedia.org/wiki/human_sacrifice_in_Aztec_culture.

[6] Klein, Christopher, The Viking Explorer Who Beat Columbus to America. htpps://www.history.com/news/the-viking-explorer-who-beat-columbus-to-america. October 2013.

[7] Ibid.

[8] Ibid.

[9] De Sanctis, Dona, Ph. D., Columbus: Fact vs. Fiction, A Report from The Order Sons of Italy in America and The Commission for Social Justice. 2002, expanded October 2005.

[10] Mary, Francis Brother F.F.I., A Handbook on Guadalupe, Catholic Spain in the Evangelization of the New World, Franciscan Friars of the Immaculate, Massachusetts 1996. Page 19.

[11] Ibid. Page 22

[12] Ibid. Pages 19 and 20.

[13] Ibid. Page 20.

[14] Ibid.

[15] Ibid. Page 21.

[16] Ibid.

[17] Ibid. Page 22.

[18] Hernandez, Bernat, History Magazine, The Cortés Conquest, http://www.nationalgeographic.com/archeology-and-history/magazine/2016/05-06/cortes-tenochtitlan. December 2018. Page 1.

[19] The dates shown are converted from the official Julian calendar, in existence before October 15, 1582, to the Gregorian calendar used thereafter.

[20] Díaz del Castillo, Bernal. Historia verdadera de la conquista de la Nueva España. Colección Autral, Espasa-Calpe, 3rd Ed., Madrid 1975.

[21] Landa, Fray Diego de, *Relacion de las cosas de Yucatán*, (Relationship of the Yucatán things) Colección Cronicas de America, Dastin, Madrid 2002. (Available on-line in Spanish as a PDF file on the website of the European Association of Mayanists.)

[22] Hernandez, Bernat, History Magazine, The Cortés Conquest, http://www.nationalgeographic.com/archeology-and-history/magazine/2016/05-06/cortes-tenochtitlan. December 2018. Page 2.

[23] Ibid.

[24] Ibid. Page 3.

[25] Cary, Diana, A Handbook on Guadalupe, Cortédiegos and the Valiant "Little Ladies", Franciscan Friars of the Immaculate, Massachusetts 1996. Page 35.

[26] Ibid.

[27] Cortés, Hernán (2005) [1523]. Cartas de relacion. Mexico: Editorial Porrua. Page 26 (English translation).

[28] Ibid.

[29] Ibid. Pages 3 & 4.

[30] Ibid. Page 4.

[31] Ibid. Page 5.

[32] Gorny, Grzegorz and Rosikon, Janusz. Guadalupe Mysteries: Deciphering the Code, San Francisco and Warsaw, 2016. Page 63.

[33] Dovas, Alexia, Why did the Aztecs Convert to Catholicism, Following the Conquest of the Spaniards in 1521. Adelphia University – Nu of New York. Lambda Alpha Journal, Volume 37, 2007. Page 65.

[34] Ibid.

[35] Ibid. Page 66.

[36] Ibid. Page 67.

[37] Ibid.

[38] Ibid. Page 69.

[39] Ibid. Page 71.

[40] Ibid.

[41] Bancroft, Hubert Howe, Volume X History of Mexico, Vol. II 1521-1600. A.L. Bancroft and Company, San Francisco, 1883. Page 175.

[42] Wood, Stephanie, Transcending Conquest: Nahua Views of Spanish Colonial Mexico, Oklahoma University Press, Oklahoma, 2003. Page 14.

[43] Ibid.

[44] Van Tuerenhout, Dirk R., Understanding Ancient Civilizations: The Aztecs-New Perspectives. ABC-CLIO, Inc. California, 2005. Page 290.

[45] Father Peter of Ghent died in 1562 after spending some forty years among the native Mesoamericans.

[46] Waldinger, María, Colonial Missionaries and Long Run Development in Mexico, London School of Economics, May 2013. Page 5.

[47] Lawrence, C.H., The Friars – The Impact of the Early Mendicant Movement on Western Society., London & New York: Longman 1994. Page 33.

[48] Waldinger, María, Colonial Missionaries and Long Run Development in Mexico, London School of Economics, May 2013. Page 9

[49] Ibid.

[50] Lawrence, C.H., The Friars – The Impact of the Early Mendicant Movement on Western Society., London & New York: Longman 1994. Page 32.

[51] Waldinger, María, Colonial Missionaries and Long Run Development in Mexico, London School of Economics, May 2013. Pages 11 & 12.

[52] Elizondo, Virgil, Guadalupe: Mother of the New Creation, Orbis Books, 1997. Page xiii.

[53] The Twelve Apostles of Mexico included Fray Martín de Valencia (the leader), Fray Francisco de Soto, Fray Martín de Coruña (also known as Fray Martín de Jesús), Fray Juan Juárez, Fray Antonio de Ciudad Rodrigo, Fray Toribio de Benavente Motolinía, García de Cisneros, Fray Luis de Fuensalida, Juan de Ribas, Fray Francisco Jiménez, Fray Andrés de Córdoba and Fray Juan de Palos.

[54] Waldinger, María, Colonial Missionaries and Long Run Development in Mexico, London School of Economics, May 2013. Page 7.

[55] Ibid.

[56] Juan Diego's pagan name was Cuauhlatohuac, but he took the name Juan Diego upon his baptism.

[57] Waldinger, María, Colonial Missionaries and Long Run Development in Mexico, London School of Economics, May 2013. Page 9.

[58] Foo, Lam Pin, How Mexico Was Conquered and Converted to Christianity. https://lampinfoo.com/2008/12/31/how-mexico-was-conquered-and-converted-to-christianity. December 2008.

[59] Johnston, Francis, The Wonder of Guadalupe, Tan Books, North Carolina 2011. Page 17.

[60] Ibid.

[61] Today the Feast of the Immaculate Conception is celebrated on December 8, but from the 5th century until the mid-19th century, it was celebrated on December 9.

[62] Johnston, Francis, The Wonder of Guadalupe, Tan Books, North Carolina 2011. Page 18.

[63] Ibid. Page 19.

[64] Elizondo, Virgil, Guadalupe: Mother of the New Creation, Orbis Books, 1997. Pages 7 & 8. NOTE: This particular translation is taken from the Nican Mopohua, a text written in the year 1545, just fourteen years after the apparition, by a Nahuatle scholar, in Nahuatle, for the Nahuatle people. It is the most precise translation available.

[64] Ibid. Page 8 & 9.

[65] Ibid. Page 8.

[66] Ibid. Page 8

[67] Ibid.

[68] Ibid.

[69] Ibid. Pages 9 & 10.

[70] Ibid. Pages 10 & 11.

[71] Ibid. Page 11.

[72] Ibid. Page 12.

[73] Johnston, Francis, The Wonder of Guadalupe, Tan Books, North Carolina 2011. Page 25.

[74] Ibid.

[75] Elizondo, Virgil, Guadalupe: Mother of the New Creation, Orbis Books, 1997. Pages 14 & 16.

[76] Ibid. Page 17.

[77] Ibid

[78] Ibid.

[79] Ibid. Page 19.

[80] Ibid. Pages 19 & 20.

[81] Ibid. Page 20.

[82] Johnston, Francis, The Wonder of Guadalupe, Tan Books, North Carolina 2011. Page 32.

[83] NOTE: Juan Bernardino could not have used the name Guadalupe since the alphabet of his native language of Nahuatl does not include the letters G and D. He must have noted a similar name which the interpreter heard as Guadalupe. Francis Johnston, author of The Wonder of Guadalupe, notes that a Marian shrine in Spain has a statue of the Virgin holding a child in one hand and a crystal scepter in the other signifying Mary's Divine Motherhood. The venerated statue was hidden in 711 AD for fear that it would be stolen or damaged in the Moorish invasion. Clergymen placed the statue in an iron casket and hid it in a cave. It wasn't until the year 1326 that Our Lady is said to have appeared to Gil Cordero and told him the exact location along the banks of the River Guadalupe, that the statue, and its authenticating documents, could be found. King Alfonso XI of Castile ordered the erection of the Royal Monastery of Guadalupe in 1340 for the purpose of displaying the statue. It was under the charge of the Franciscans. It became the most celebrated shrine in Spain and was the place where Christopher Columbus prayed prior to embarking on his journey of discovery. After surviving a shipwreck, Columbus also named the island that saved him Guadalupe. The early Spanish missionaries, therefore, naturally had a great devotion to the Virgin of Guadalupe. That is why the interpreter may have mistaken Juan Bernardino's words as "the Ever-Virgin Holy Mary of Guadalupe." For many years the native people refused to call the image Guadalupe,

referring to it instead by pseudo-pagan names such as Tonantzin. The name Guadalupe does not show itself in early texts such as the Inan Huey Tlamahuizoltzin which historians believe predated the Nican Mopohua. There is substantial historical evidence that the Lady identified herself as Tequantlaxopeuh (pronounced Tequetalope) translated into "Who saves us from the Devourer." At the time, the Devourer was representative of Satan, meaning that the Virgin was really identifying herself as the Immaculate Conception, the One who vanquish Satan. In fact, when Bishop Zumárraga wrote to Cortés on December 24, 1531 to invite him to the procession of the sacred image from the capital to the first hermitage, he referred to the image as the Immaculate Conception. Eventually, the name Immaculate Conception was changed to Guadalupe. In 1895, after an intense study of the word Guadalupe, Professor D. Mariano Jacabo Rojas, head of the department of Nahuatle in the National Museum of Archaeology, History and Ethnography, determined that the Virgin actually used the word Coatlaxopeuh, which means "she who breaks, stamps or crushes the serpent." This too is the equivalent of the Immaculate Conception. This study was corroborated by two independent authorities in 1936 and 1953.

[84] Gorny, Grzegorz and Rosikon, Janusz. Guadalupe Mysteries: Deciphering the Code, San Francisco and Warsaw, 2016. Page 36.

[85] Johnston, Francis, The Wonder of Guadalupe, Tan Books, North Carolina 2011. Page 41.

[86] Wahlig, Dr. Charles, Guadalupe in Spain, A Handbook on Guadalupe, Catholic Spain in the Evangelization of the New World, Franciscan Friars of the Immaculate, Massachusetts 1996. Page 24.

[87] Ibid. Page 24.

[88] Ibid. Page 25.

[89] Johnston, Francis, The Wonder of Guadalupe, Tan Books, North Carolina 2011. Page 47.

[90] Ibid.

[91] Johnston, Francis, The Wonder of Guadalupe, Tan Books, North Carolina 2011. Page 48.

[92] Ibid. Page 51.

[93] Ibid.

[94] Ibid.

[95] Ibid. Page 53.

[96] Ibid.

[97] Ibid. Page 56.

[98] Ibid.

[99] Ibid. Page 56 & 57.

[100] Ibid. Page 57.

[101] Ibid. Page 58.

[102] Ibid. Page 57.

[103] Ibid. Page 58.

[104] Ibid.

[105] Gorny, Grzegorz and Rosikon, Janusz. Guadalupe Mysteries: Deciphering the Code, San Francisco and Warsaw, 2016. Page 51.

[106] Ibid. Page 52

[107] Ibid. Page 5.

[108] Ibid. Page 53.

[109] Garibay, Angel M. Monsignor, A Handbook on Guadalupe, The Spiritual Motherhood of Mary, Franciscan Friars of the Immaculate, Massachusetts 1996. Page 10.

[110] Ibid. Page 16.

[111] Gorny, Grzegorz and Rosikon, Janusz. Guadalupe Mysteries: Deciphering the Code, San Francisco and Warsaw, 2016. Page 5.

[112] Ibid. Page 36.

[113] Ibid. Page 42.

[114] Ibid.

[115] Ibid. Page 54.

[116] Ibid. Page 54.

[117] Ibid. Page 55.

[118] Ibid. Pages 58 & 60.

[119] Ibid. Page 61.

[120] Ibid. Page 63 and 68.

[121] Castellano, Daniel J. Historiography of the Apparition of Guadalupe, http://www.arcaneknowledge.org/catholic/guadalupe12.htm, Part XII. Page 10.

[122] Ibid. Page 11.

[123] Ibid. Page 10.

[124] Eduardo Chávez, Our Lady of Guadalupe and Saint Juan Diego: The Historical Evidence, New York and Toronto, 2006. Page 27.

[125] Castellano, Daniel J. Historiography of the Apparition of Guadalupe, http://www.arcaneknowledge.org/catholic/guadalupe12.htm, Part XII. Page 13.

[126] Ibid. Page 14.

[127] Ibid.

[128] Ibid.

[129] Ibid. Page 15

[130] Ibid. Page 16.

[131] Ibid.

[132] Ibid. Page 17.

[133] Ibid.

[134] Ibid.

[135] Ibid.

[136] Ibid. Page 19.

[137] Ibid.

[138] Ibid. Page 21.

[139] Johnston, Francis, The Wonder of Guadalupe, Tan Books, North Carolina 2011. Page 131.

[140] Mexican forensic scientist Ernesto Sodi Pallares, who devoted much of his career to the investigation of the tilma, provides the only definite source of information on the 1936 study. He does this through personal testimony to fellow researcher Manuel de la Mora Ojega. That testimony was published in 1980, three years after the death of Pallares, in a document entitled *Descubrimento de un Busto Humano en los Ojos de la Virgen de Guadalupe*.

[141] Castellano, Daniel J. Historiography of the Apparition of Guadalupe, http://www.arcaneknowledge.org/catholic/guadalupe12.htm, Part XIII. Page 11.

[142] Ibid.

[143] Ibid. Page 12.

[144] Ibid.

[145] Castellano, Daniel J. Historiography of the Apparition of Guadalupe, http://www.arcaneknowledge.org/catholic/guadalupe12.htm, Part XIII. Page 14.

[146] The experiment indicated to Wilhelmy that "most of the face was still original, except for retouches on the forehead, nose, cheekbone, and tip of the chin. These were perhaps justified by the darkening caused by candle smoke in the upper part of the image. Similarly, he saw that the cloak, though mostly original, had been retouched in the area of the head. Through a blue filter, he could discern a horizontal line, curved downward, of a change in tone, probably corresponding to where the crown had once been. He also saw a reddish spike extending from the apparent crown, matching a color found in some of the surrounding rays, which were now mostly overlaid with gold." - From http://www.arcaneknowledge.org/catholic/guadalupe12.htm, Part XIII, page 15.

Further, Francis Johnston notes that the theory that significant alterations may have been made to the image is simply untenable. We have a painting of the image from 1570 that the Archbishop of Mexico commissioned for King Phillip II of Spain. That painting, which was presented to Admiral Andrea Doria who carried it into the battle of Lepanto in 1571, shows exactly what appeared on the image as of 1570, only 39 years after the tilma was unfurled by Juan Diego. That painting shows the image exactly as it appears today. Over the subsequent years, any alterations that may have been made to the image, such as adding a border of cherubs or shortening the fingers to make the Virgin appear more Mexican, have been washed off or faded out of the image.

From Francis Johnston's The Wonder of Guadalupe, Tan Books, Charlotte, North Carolina, 1981.

[147] Castellano, Daniel J. Historiography of the Apparition of Guadalupe, http://www.arcaneknowledge.org/catholic/guadalupe12.htm, Part XIII. Page 15

[148] Ibid.

[149] Ibid. Page 17. "these areas (i.e., of the now erased roses and cherubim) have been painted over."

[150] Ibid. Page 19.

[151] Ibid.

[152] Ibid.

[153] Ibid. Page 20.

[154] Gorny, Grzegorz and Rosikon, Janusz. Guadalupe Mysteries: Deciphering the Code, Ignatius Press, San Francisco and Rosikon Press, Warsaw, 2016. Page 234.

[155] Our Lady of Guadalupe, Patroness of the Americas – Website. The Mystery in Our Lady's Eyes, https://www.sancta.org/eyes.html. Page 1.

[156] Ibid.

[157] Gorny, Grzegorz and Rosikon, Janusz. Guadalupe Mysteries: Deciphering the Code, Ignatius Press, San Francisco and Rosikon Press, Warsaw, 2016. Page 237.

[158] Johnston, Francis, The Wonder of Guadalupe, Tan Books, North Carolina 2011. Page 131.

[159] Castellano, Daniel J. Historiography of the Apparition of Guadalupe, http://www.arcaneknowledge.org/catholic/guadalupe12.htm, Part XIII. Page 20

[160] Ibid. Page 21

[161] Ibid.

[162] Ibid. Page 2.

[163] Johnston, Francis, The Wonder of Guadalupe, Tan Books, North Carolina 2011. Pages 131 - 132.

[164] Ibid. Pages 132 - 133.

[165] Ibid. Page 133.

[166] Ibid. Pages 138 – 139.

[167] Gorny, Grzegorz and Rosikon, Janusz. Guadalupe Mysteries: Deciphering the Code, Ignatius Press, San Francisco and Rosikon Press, Warsaw, 2016. Page 238.

[168] Ibid. Page 240.

[169] Ibid.

[170] Johnston, Francis, The Wonder of Guadalupe, Tan Books, North Carolina 2011. Page 141.

[171] Ibid. Page 142.

[172] Ibid.

[173] Ibid.

[174] Ibid.

[175] Zenit Staff, Science Stunned by Virgin of Guadalupe's Eyes: Engineer Sees a Reflection, Literally, From a Scene in 1531. https://zenit.org/articles/science-stunned-by-virgin-of-guadalupe-s-eyes/. Rome, January 14, 2001. Page 1.

[176] Johnston, Francis, The Wonder of Guadalupe, Tan Books, North Carolina 2011. Page 143.

[177] Ibid.

[178] Ibid. Page 144.

[179] Ibid. Page 145.

[180] Gorny, Grzegorz and Rosikon, Janusz. Guadalupe Mysteries: Deciphering the Code, Ignatius Press, San Francisco and Rosikon Press, Warsaw, 2016. Page 212.

[181] Gorny, Grzegorz and Rosikon, Janusz. Guadalupe Mysteries: Deciphering the Code, Ignatius Press, San Francisco and Rosikon Press, Warsaw, 2016. Pages 55 & 56.

[182] Ibid. Page 215.

[183] Ibid. Page 224.

[184] Ibid.

[185] Ibid. Pages 227 & 228.

[186] Ibid. Pages 204 & 207.

[187] Ibid. Pages 208 & 211.

[188] Ibid. Page 212.

[189] Zenit Staff, Science Stunned by Virgin of Guadalupe's Eyes: Engineer Sees a Reflection, Literally, From a Scene in 1531. https://zenit.org/articles/science-stunned-by-virgin-of-guadalupe-s-eyes/. Rome, January 14, 2001. Page 1.

[190] Ibid. Pages 1 and 2.

[191] Gorny, Grzegorz and Rosikon, Janusz. Guadalupe Mysteries: Deciphering the Code, Ignatius Press, San Francisco and Rosikon Press, Warsaw, 2016. Pages 247 - 248.

[192] https://zenit.org/articles/science-stunned-by-virgin-of-guadalupe-s-eyes/. Rome, January 14, 2001. Page 2.

[193] Gorny, Grzegorz and Rosikon, Janusz. Guadalupe Mysteries: Deciphering the Code, Ignatius Press, San Francisco and Rosikon Press, Warsaw, 2016. Page 243.

[194] Lynch, Dan, The Amazing Truth of Our Lady of Guadalupe, Catholic Exchange, December 2002. www.catholiceducation.org/en/culture/catholic-contributions/the-amazing-truth-of-our-lady-of-guadalupe-html. Page 1.

[195] Garibay, Angel M. Monsignor, A Handbook on Guadalupe, "The Spiritual Motherhood of Mary," Franciscan Friars of the Immaculate, Massachusetts 1996. Page 64.

[196] Lynch, Dan, The Amazing Truth of Our Lady of Guadalupe, Catholic Exchange, December 2002. www.catholiceducation.org/en/culture/catholic-contributions/the-amazing-truth-of-our-lady-of-guadalupe-html. Page 2.

[197] Ibid.

[198] The New American Bible, Translated from the Original Languages with Critical Use of All the Ancient Sources, Revelation Chapter 12, verses 1-2. Oxford Press, New York. Page 2112.

[199] See https://www.bbc.com/news/world-us-canada-47066307, https://www.cbsnews.com/news/virginia-abortion-bill-proposed-by-kathy-tran-third-trimester-today-2019-01-30/, and http://nymag.com/intelligencer/2019/01/no-virginia-democrats-dont-support-infanticide.html.

[200] Pavone, Fr. Frank, Our Lady of Guadalupe and the Pro-life Movement, Priests for Life Website, Educational Resources. https//www.priestsfor-life.org/articles/2791-our-lady-of-guadalupe-and-the-pro-life-movement. Page 1.

[201] Ibid. Page 2.

[202] Garibay, Angel M. Monsignor, A Handbook on Guadalupe, "The Spiritual Motherhood of Mary," Franciscan Friars of the Immaculate, Massachusetts 1996. Page 144.

[203] Ibid. Pages 2 & 3.

[204] Knights of Columbus, Our Lady of Guadalupe, 2018-2019, Page 1. http://www.guadalupebook.com/gb/en/other/kofc_page.html.

[205] Ibid.

[206] Columbia Magazine On-line, A publication of the Knights of Columbus, New Haven, CT., 2014, Page 1. http://www.guadalupecelebration.com/gc/en/kc/index.html.

[207] Mahoney, Karen, Knights Silver Rose Promotes Our Lady of Guadalupe, Respect for Human Life, As It Passes Through Diocese, The Catholic Sun, Anthem, AZ. Page 2. https://catholicsun.org/2016/10/29/knights-silver-rose-promotes-our-lady-of-guadalupe.

[208] Gorny, Grzegorz and Rosikon, Janusz. Guadalupe Mysteries: Deciphering the Code, Ignatius Press, San Francisco and Rosikon Press, Warsaw, 2016. Page 229.

[209] Ibid. Page 228.

[210] While the Miracle Hunter Website calls him Fr. William Schulenberg, both the NY Times and the Washington Post refer to him as Msgr. Guillermo Schulenberg Prado.

PHOTO CREDITS:

Page 37- AlejandroLinaresGarcia [CC BY-SA 4.0 (https://creativecommons.org/licenses/by-sa/4.0)]

Page 48 - Enrique López-Tamayo Biosca [CC BY 2.0 (https://creativecommons.org/li-censes/by/2.0)]

Page 52 - Joaquín Martínez Rosado [CC BY-SA 3.0 (https://creativecommons.org/licenses/by-sa/3.0)]

Page 146 - Photos courtesy of Citizens for a Pro-Life Society   www.prolifesociety.com

Page 147 – Photo courtesy of The Center for Bio-Ethical Reform.

About the Author

Historian Paul F. Caranci is Rhode Island's former Deputy Secretary of State. He dedicated his life to public service, history and writing. In addition to his nine published books, Caranci's articles have appeared in a plethora of magazines and on-line news services. He has written two award-winning books; *Scoundrels: Defining Corruption Through Tales of Political Intrigue in Rhode Island* (Winner of the Dorry Award for Non-Fiction Book of the Year, 2016), and *The Hanging and Redemption of John Gordon: The True Story of Rhode Island's Last Execution* (Selected by the *Providence Journal* as one of the top five non-fiction books of the 2013). In addition, *The Promise of Fatima: One Hundred Years of History, Mystery, and Faith* was named a finalist in the International Book Awards in 2017. Likewise, *I am the Immaculate Conception: The Story of Bernadette of Lourdes*, was named a finalist in the International Book Awards in 2018.

Paul serves on the Board of Directors of the Association of Rhode Island Authors (ARIA) and the Rhode Island Publications Society. He is a co-founder of The Municipal Heritage Group. He is also a former member of the Heritage Harbor Museum Board of Directors, the RI Heritage Hall of Fame Board of Directors, and the Board of Directors of the American Diabetes Association – Rhode Island Affiliate. He served on the Board of Directors of the Diabetes Foundation of Rhode Island for sixteen years serving as its Chairman for two of those years.

Paul is married to his childhood sweetheart, Margie. The couple has two adult children, Heather and Matthew, and four grandsons, Matthew Jr., Jacob, Vincent and Casey. They reside in Rhode Island.

This is his tenth book.

Also by the Author...

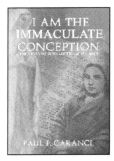 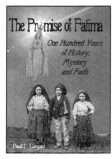 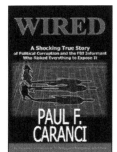 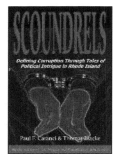

   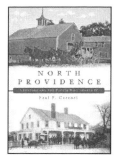

*Available at online retailers, bookstores
and www.StillwaterPress.com*

*Paul Caranci is available to speak at your conference or function,
or to your civic, church, political, or ethnic group or club.
You may contact him at*

municipalheritage@gmail.com

www.PaulCaranci.com

ORDER FORM

Please use the following to order additional copies of:

1. Heavenly Portrait: The Miraculous Image of Our Lady of Guadalupe **($20.00)**
2. I Am the Immaculate Conception: The Story of St. Bernadette and Her Apparitions at Lourdes **($20.00)**
3. The Promise of Fatima: One Hundred Years of History, Mystery & Faith **($20.00)**
4. Wired: A Shocking True Story of Political Corruption and the FBI Informant Who Risked Everything to Expose It **($23.00)**
5. Scoundrels: Defining Political Corruption Through Tales of Political Intrigue in Rhode Island **($20.00)**
6. Monumental Providence: Legends of History in Sculpture, Statuary, Monuments and Memorials **($20.00)**
7. The Essential Guide to Running for Local Office **($15.00)**
8. The Hanging & Redemption of John Gordon: The True Story of Rhode Island's Last Execution **($20.00)**
9. North Providence: A History & The People Who Shaped It **($20.00)**
10. Award Winning Real Estate in a Depressed or Declining Market **($10.00)**

_____ (QTY) _____(Title) X _____ (Price) = $_____

_____ (QTY) _____(Title) X _____ (Price) = $_____

_____ (QTY) _____(Title) X _____ (Price) = $_____

_____ (QTY) _____(Title) X _____ (Price) = $_____

_____ (QTY) _____(Title) X _____ (Price) = $_____

Total for books $_____ + Postage** $_____ = **TOTAL COST** $_____

**Postage: Please add $3.00 for the first book and $1.50 for each additional book ordered.

Payment Method:

___ Personal Check Enclosed (Payable to **M. Caranci Books**)

___ Charge my Credit Card

Name:_____ BILLING ZIP CODE:_____

Visa_____ Master Card_____

Card Number:_____ EXP:_____/_____CSC (3 digit code) _____

Signature:_____

Ship My Book To:

Name _____

Street _____

City _____State:_____Zip:_____

Phone _____Email:_____

MAIL YOUR COMPLETED FORM TO:
Paul F. Caranci
26 East Avenue
North Providence, RI 02911

You may also order using my Email address at municipalheritage@gmail.com or by calling me at 401-639-4502

Please visit my Website at www.paulcaranci.com

Made in the
USA
Middletown, DE

76082565R00119